Cole Aeslen.

A BOOK OF BRIT

An Anthology of Words and Pictures

THE golden sunshine crept upon my book
And changed the pages to diminishing fields,
The words to bushes where the thrushes sang.
I wandered back where I had been before,
Page after page, enchanted with the grass,
The flowering hedgerow and the scented branch,
The rills with voice of linnets, and the birds
With music as of hidden waters tumbling
Through stones and mosses into secret pools.
I looked upon the wisest words again
And saw the sowers at their ancient work
Along the furrows gleaming through the clay.
The seed of thought, and seed for human bread,
Eternal beauty and immediate need,
Were scattered there before my hungry eyes
In that inspired confusion of the sun.

RICHARD CHURCH
The Glance Backward, 1930

FOR MY MOTHER

A BOOK OF

BRITAIN

AN ANTHOLOGY

OF WORDS AND PICTURES

COMPILED BY

JOHN HADFIELD

1957

LONDON: HULTON PRESS

FIRST PUBLISHED IN 1956

E. HULTON & CO. LTD.

161/166 FLEET STREET

LONDON E.C.4

PRINTED IN GREAT BRITAIN BY

THE CURWEN PRESS

LONDON

REPRINTED 1957

REPRINTED 1959

INTRODUCTION

THIS BOOK IS NOT, perhaps, quite what its title might suggest. Readers will look in vain for Wordsworth's daffodils, for views of Windsor Castle and Clovelly, or for solemn appraisals of the British way of life. Here is a purely personal choice of poetry, prose and pictures which reflect one man's feelings for his native land.

There was a time when it would have been slightly embarrassing to admit, in so many words, that one loved one's country. Recently, however, the experience of having it very nearly stolen from under our feet has made us less self-conscious at owning the sentiment. At moments of stress or hazard between 1939 and 1945 there appeared to the mind's eye certain scenes and vistas which seemed to have a desperate sentimental value. In this book I have tried to recapture the inspiration and consolation of such moments.

Love of country has certain parallels with the love of a man for a woman. Beauty is an element in it, but not the all-important one. A man may be drawn to a woman by perfection of feature or figure, as he is attracted to the Wye Valley by the view at Symonds Yat. It is doubtful, however, whether many men want to make their home by Symonds Yat. Just as the enduring love of man and woman is stirred by a mere turn of the head or a footfall on the stairs, so the deep attachment of man to his native place can be reawakened by such homely sights as the mist rising from water meadows or the first blush of apple blossom in a suburban street.

In this book will be found a good many passages of verse and prose which are unspectacular and unhallowed by earlier anthologists. By my exclusion of Wordsworth's daffodils, Browning's home-thoughts, or Shakespeare's 'precious stone set in the silver sea' I am not belittling such esteemed pieces – indeed, they have never ceased to thrill me as they did when I was a child. The inspiration of the

British scene, however, has, especially during the past two hundred years, been felt very keenly at all levels of poetic and artistic achievement. There is a vast literature of British topographical attachment, just as there must be many acres of canvas and drawing paper covered with tributes to the British landscape. I have found it very rewarding to delve into quarto poems by eighteenth-century parsons, back-numbers of *The Sporting Magazine*, or volumes of local piety printed at such places as Dorchester, Sudbury or Peebles.

I do not suggest that most of my material has come from such sources. There is, I think, poetry and prose in this book, by authors as far apart in time as George Peele and Sir Osbert Sitwell, which would be worthy of inclusion in any Golden Treasury of English landscape literature. But the unending delight of quarrying in this ground is that one may at any time, in even the least promising seams, come upon flashes of pure gold. 'The air is full of ballad notes,' wrote Andrew Lang. Again and again some half-forgotten poet – Ebenezer Elliott, James Hurdis, David Gray, Thomas Double-day, Ebenezer Jones, or currently unfashionable writers of the recent past such as Austin Dobson or John Drinkwater – proves how landscape can inspire rare felicities of phrase and lyrical perception.

It is the lyrical response to the British scene with which I have concerned myself. I have avoided, for the most part, the grand manner and the generalization, just as the selection of illustrations avoids the panoramic view, cloud capp'd towers, castles and cathedrals. So often, in English lyrical writing, the detail is a greater inspiration than the whole. The reason for this, I suggest, lies in the scale and nature of the English landscape.

With the exception of a few thousand acres in the Fells or on Dartmoor, the landscape of England is man-made, tamed, humanized and reduced from the awe-inspiring scale of Nature to proportions manageable alike by the landscape gardener, the farmer, the lyric poet, and the water-colourist. The first two have transformed it from Nature's indiscipline into pattern and order, with the result that the water-colourist has his vista ready-shaped for the sketch-book, and the poet finds his material set out in sonnet lengths.

English landscape writing, however, frequently rises beyond the scale of its subject matter. Attention to detail, to Crabbe's 'bright varnish of the morning dew', or to Mr Blunden's 'round leaf, shield leaf, patterned spray', often leads on to poetic awareness of 'the skies of history hurrying overhead'.

One could develop the same argument in regard to the artists, and I hope this may be shown by my choice of illustrations, which deliberately range from a simple Staffordshire pottery chimney-piece ornament to the classical splendour of Richard Wilson's Snowdon. It may seem, for instance, that the paintings of Mr Ivon Hitchens are mere colour, poured on to his canvas with intuitive, lyrical abandon. In fact, Mr Hitchens is a most intellectual painter, and the composition of his pictures is worked out with almost mathematical care.

The capacity of English painters to take a limited, familiar scene, and confer upon it transcendant values, is perfectly expressed by Mr Day Lewis's lines on Constable:

> His sunburst inspiration
> Made earthly forms so true
> To life, so new to vision,
> That now the actual view
> Seems a mere phantom, through
> Whose blur we glimpse creation.

As in the two earlier anthologies which I have compiled to this pattern I have not attempted to explain my sequence of ideas. I hope it will become apparent to those who read with attention that each section seeks to present a coherent argument, and that words and pictures are deliberately related, though often differing widely in style, period and subject. Each reader must interpret the book in his or her own way.

In the geographical nature of our island the section entitled 'Seascape' must take the first place. Under the heading 'Landscape' I have tried to show the inter-relation of man and nature that has characterized the British scene from the 'roofless past' to the Virginia-creeper-clad present. 'Figures in a Landscape' develops this theme by showing a glimpse or two of Merry England and of men at work.

I have already indicated the part played in this book by the section called 'Detail'. This leads on to consideration of what I regard as two of the most notable British art-forms – sport and gardening. In the concluding section, 'Street Scene', I have tried to suggest – there is no space to do more – the lyrical impulse reacting to the urban scene, not with the easy assurance of a Canaletto painting St Paul's, but with that strange blend of romance and precision with which Mr L. S. Lowry translates the back-street scene in Lancashire.

Mr Lowry's vision seems to me, in his special field, to be surprisingly akin to that of John Clare in quite another field. To have brought their work together in one book, and set it beside that of, for instance, Van Dyck, Mr Betjeman, Francis Quarles and the author of an anonymous coster song, has meant for me a singularly happy and eventful walk through the highways, alleys, lanes and footpaths of British landscape art and letters. If the result may seem to some to be a curiously patterned patchwork, I can only plead that the British landscape is like that, and I am quite ready to admit, in the words of one of the most lovely poems in this book:

I have lost my way, and found my heart.

J. H.

CONTENTS

NOTE. *The reference at the end of each passage is, in almost every instance, to the date and place of its first appearance in book form. The spelling and punctuation of the text has been modernized throughout, except in the passage about Chatsworth on page 203. In order to allow as much room as possible for the illustrations, notes on their sources are printed at the end of the book.*

LET us not be grudging, or falsely modest, about the graces of this island. We are the luckiest of races in our surroundings, whatever we may think of our destiny in other respects. We can love Nature without being abashed or archaic. We come after generation on generation of Englishmen in every rank of birth and ability who have shown us the way. Such a profusion of estates and farms and cottages and commons and field paths was never given us without a deep and tranquil faith. So vast a range of prose and verse of natural piety was not the product of romantic eccentricity. So enchanting an English garden was brought to bloom with a certainty of manly understanding. Our painters have failed to compete with the world-masters of myth and allegory – but they did not waste time, while they sat in ten thousand leafy look-outs and caught the warm shower stealing and giving odours on the sunny labyrinths, or the last messages of light between the village walls and the summer sun. Our shepherds never doubted, as they shifted their hurdles or came to the fair, that earth had something of heaven in it. Our naturalists have not been driven away from their endless scrutiny by any desperate conjecture that life should be more exciting. This is the country of Arthur Young and William Cobbett, of the poets of *Polyolbion* and *The Seasons*, of Cotman and de Wint, of White of Selborne and Harrison of Ightham, of Loudon and Paxton and Anne Pratt and Frank Buckland; the country of a nameless multitude who have spent their lives in making Nature their friend, and have not thrown a bridge across a stream or made a hovel for farm carts without an instinctive compact with their friend.

EDMUND BLUNDEN, *Votive Tablets*, 1931

SEASCAPE

Is it not because it is always moving, and because one is not moving with it that the sea means so much more to one than any possible inland scenery? A tree, a meadow, though it grows and changes, grows and changes imperceptibly; I cannot see it in motion; it seems to be always there, irritatingly immobile. But the sea is always moving past me; it is like a friend who comes and goes and is faithful; its motion is all I have to give me some sense of permanency in a world where all things grow old and pass away, except the sea. Byron was right, though he spoke pompously: 'Time writes no wrinkle on thine azure brow'. Every part of the earth's body is growing old, and shows the signs and scars of age; only the sea is without that symptom of mortality, and remains a witness to the original youth of creation.

ARTHUR SYMONS, *Cities and Sea-Coasts and Islands*, 1918

OH, I do like to be beside the seaside;
I do like to be beside the sea:
I do like to stroll upon the Prom, Prom, Prom,
Where the brass bands play, tiddely-om-pom-pom!
So just let me be beside the seaside:
I'll be beside myself with glee;
And there's lots of girls, beside,
I should like to be beside,
Beside the seaside, beside the sea.

JOHN A. GLOVER-KIND,
Beside the Seaside, 1909

13

NAVAL VIEWS

IN going across the harbour we passed close under the stern of the old *Royal George*. It was the first time I ever floated on salt water; the first hundred-gun ship I ever saw. Ye gods! what a sight – what a sensation! . . . It is impossible to forget the breathless astonishment and delight with which my eyes were fixed upon this ship. Nothing so exquisitely touching has ever occurred to me since to produce the same frantic joy. After the first exclamation of ecstasy I for a time spoke not a word; overwhelmed by a thousand feelings, and almost motionless, until presently, as we approached nearer to the *Royal George*, and went closely under her richly carved stern, I broke into a rapid succession of questions, and almost springing out of the hands of the strokesman of the boat, who held me as I stood upon the seat, I was told I should tumble into the sea if I was not quiet. . . .

I remember old John Allen, who had been Sir Samuel Hood's coxswain when commodore in America, and then in the same capacity in my father's boat, said, 'I see, sir, you are already determined to be a sailor.' He never spoke a truer word.

ADMIRAL SIR THOMAS BYAM MARTIN, *Journal*, 1781

WE sail at dusk. The red moon,
Rising in a paper lantern, sets fire
To the water; the black headland disappears,
Sullen in shadow, clenched like a paw.

The docks grow flat, rubbered with mist.
Cranes, like tall drunks, hang
Over the railway. The unloading of coal
Continues under blue arc-lights.

Turning south, the moon like a rouged face
Between masts, the knotted aerials swing
Taut against the horizon, the bag
Of sea crumpled in the spray-flecked blackness.

Towards midnight the cold stars, high
Over Europe, freeze on the sky,
Stigmata above the flickering lights
Of Holland. Flashes of gunfire

Lick out over meditative coastlines, betraying
The stillness. Taking up position, night falls
Exhausted about us. The wakes
Of gunboats sew the green dark with speed.

From Dunkirk red flames open fanwise
In spokes of light; like the rising moon
Setting fire to the sky, the remote
Image of death burns on the water.

The slow muffle of hours. Clouds grow visible.
Altering course the moon congeals on a new
Bearing. Northwards again, and Europe recedes
With the first sharp splinters of dawn.

The orange sky lies over the harbour,
Derricks and pylons like scarecrows
Black in the early light. And minesweepers
Pass us, moving out slowly to the North Sea.

ALAN ROSS, *Something of the Sea*, 1954

THE HOLLOW OAK

Is she not beautiful? reposing there
    On her own shadow, with her white wings furled;
Moveless, as in the sleepy sunny air,
    Rests the meek swan in her own quiet world.

Is she not beautiful? her graceful bow
    Triumphant rising o'er th' enamour'd tides
That, glittering in the noon-day sunbeam, now
    Just leap and die along her polished sides . . .

NOEL THOMAS CARRINGTON
My Native Village and Other Poems, 1830

THERE's tempest in yon horned moon,
And lightning in yon cloud;
And hark the music, mariners!
The wind is wakening loud –
The wind is wakening loud, my boys,
The lightning flashes free:
The hollow oak our palace is,
Our heritage the sea.

ALLAN CUNNINGHAM
The Songs of Scotland, 1825

NELSON'S FLAGSHIPS (DETAIL): PAINTING BY NICHOLAS POCOCK, 1807

SIGNALS: PAINTING BY EDWARD WADSWORTH, 1942

As for honour, who knows not (that knows anything) that in all records of late times of actions chronicled to the everlasting fame and renown of this Kingdom, still the naval part is the thread that runs through the whole wooft, the burden of the song, the scope of the text?

JOHN HOLLOND, *First Discourse of the Navy*, 1638

THE first article of an Englishman's political creed must be, that he believeth in the sea. . . . We are in an island, confined to it by God Almighty, not as a penalty but a grace, and one of the greatest that can be given to mankind. Happy confinement, that hath made us free, rich, and quiet; a fair portion in this world, and very well worth the preserving; a figure that ever hath been envied, and could never be imitated, by our neighbours.

GEORGE SAVILE, MARQUESS OF HALIFAX
A Rough Draft of a New Model at Sea, 1694

BRITAIN is known to be the most flourishing and excellent, most renowned and famous isle of the whole world, so rich in commodities, so beautiful in situation, so resplendent in all glory, that if the most Omnipotent had fashioned the world round like a ring, as he did like a globe, it might have been most worthily the only gem therein. . . . It is walled and guarded by the ocean, most commodious for traffic to all parts of the world, and watered with pleasant, fishful and navigable rivers, which yield safe havens and roads, and furnished with shipping and sailors, that it may rightly be termed the Lady of the Sea.

WILLIAM CAMDEN, *Britannia*, 1586
translated by Philemon Holland, 1610

THE BEAUTY OF THE SHIP

WHEN I saw her first, there was a smoke of mist about her as high as her foreyard. Her topsails and flying kites had a faint glow upon them where the dawn caught them. Then the mist rolled away from her, so that we could see her hull and the glimmer of the red sidelight as it was hoisted inboard. She was rolling slightly, tracing an arc against the heaven, and as I watched her the glow upon her deepened, till every sail she wore burned rosily like an opal turned to the sun, like a fiery jewel. She was radiant, she was of an immortal beauty, that swaying, delicate clipper. Coming as she came, out of the mist into the dawn, she was like a spirit, like an intellectual presence. Her hull glowed; her rails glowed; there was colour upon the boats and tackling. She was a lofty ship (with skysails and royal staysails) and it was wonderful to watch her blushing in the sun, swaying and curveting. She was alive with a more than mortal life. One thought that she would speak in some strange language or break out into music which would express the sea and that great flower in the sky. She came trembling down to us, rising up high and plunging; showing the red lead below her water-line; then diving down till the smother bubbled over her hawseholes. She bowed and curveted; the light caught the skylights on the poop; she gleamed and sparkled; she shook the sea from her as she rose. There was no man aboard of us but was filled with the beauty of that ship.

JOHN MASEFIELD, *A Tarpaulin Muster*, 1907

Succefs to the Great Brittain of the Main
With may She Stem the turrant of the Main
Great Succefs and Safe Return aGain
A. STAFFELL

VERPOOL DELFT PUNCH BOWL, c. 1760

FEBRUARY IN THE ISLE OF WIGHT: PAINTING BY JOHN BRETT, A.R.A., 1866

THE WELCOME OF THE COAST

A WEEK afterwards the *Narcissus* entered the chops of the Channel. Under white wings she skimmed low over the blue sea like a great tired bird speeding to its nest. The clouds raced with her mastheads; they rose astern enormous and white, soared to the zenith, flew past, and, falling down the wide curve of the sky, seemed to dash headlong into the sea – the clouds swifter than the ship, more free, but without a home. The coast to welcome her stepped out of space into the sunshine. The lofty headlands trod masterfully into the sea; the wide bays smiled in the light; the shadows of homeless clouds ran along the sunny plains, leaped over valleys, without a check darted up the hills, rolled down the slopes; and the sunshine pursued them with patches of running brightness. On the brows of dark cliffs white lighthouses shone in pillars of light. The Channel glittered like a blue mantle shot with gold and starred by the silver of the capping seas. The *Narcissus* rushed past the headlands and the bays. Outward-bound vessels crossed her track, lying over, and with their masts stripped for a slogging fight with the hard sou'wester. And, inshore, a string of smoking steamboats waddled, hugging the coast, like migrating and amphibious monsters, distrustful of the restless waves.

At night the headlands retreated, the bays advanced into one unbroken line of gloom. The lights of the earth mingled with the lights· of heaven; and above the tossing lanterns of a trawling fleet a great lighthouse shone steadily, like an enormous riding light burning above a vessel of fabulous dimensions. Below its steady glow, the coast, stretching away straight and black, resembled the high side of an indestructible craft riding motionless upon the immortal and unresting sea. The dark land lay alone in the midst of waters, like a mighty ship bestarred with vigilant lights – a ship carrying the burden of millions of lives – a ship freighted with dross and with jewels, with gold and with steel. She towered up immense and strong, guarding priceless traditions and untold suffering, sheltering glorious memories and base forgetfulness, ignoble virtues and splendid transgressions. A great ship! For ages had the ocean battered in vain her enduring sides; she was there when the world was vaster and darker, when the sea was great and mysterious, and ready to surrender the prize of fame to audacious men. A ship mother of fleets and nations! The great flagship of the race, stronger than the storms, and anchored in the open sea.

JOSEPH CONRAD, *The Nigger of the 'Narcissus'*, 1898

THE LIGHTS of the Goodwins came twinkling on, a little uncertainly at first, as if they were not quite sure they were wanted. Away on the right, the pier put on its little coloured spangle of lights, which dropped long trembling reflections into the water. On the cliff to the left our neighbouring town turned itself into a bracelet of glimmering yellow points. The whole traffic of the sea became a pattern of lights, fixed or wandering, in a mystery of purple air and indigo waters. You saw something that looked like a distant row of houses on the move and you knew that a liner from Calcutta or the Cape had passed by and that hundreds of your fellow-countrymen were staring over the rails and hearing the great engines go humming, *Home-in-the-morning, Home-in-the-morning*. And little lights, as lonely as a few fireflies in a desert, crept by, going the other way, and you knew that a tramp or two had slipped out of the Thames, bound perhaps for Monte Video or Callao.

J. B. PRIESTLEY, *The Balconinny*, 1929

LONDON RIVER

AND in the evening, a little after sunset, you may enjoy what I judge to be the most lovely experience in London – the journey through the dusk from Wapping to Westminster. There are not many lights in the Pool; the warehouses are dark, become dignified and mysterious, palaces, fortresses, or temples. The starboard light of a steamer coming up on the flood round the bend astern of you is a brilliant emerald, the eye of some pursuing monster; she sends her final hoot of warning to the Tower Bridge, the thrilling announcement that another ship has come home; the Tower Bridge is a colourless outline, a children's toy, against the faint rose of the western sky, and St. Paul's dome, beyond, is only the ghost of a dome. Lighted buses are congregated on the bridge, waiting reverently for the ship to pass, and suddenly the road divides, the great arms of the bridge rise up and pronounce a blessing on you while your impudent craft scuttles through ahead of the steamer, as if the bascules had been lifted for you.

There are more lights now: London Bridge wears a moving frieze of light, and we have come back to the roar of traffic. The bridges come thick and fast – Cannon Street and Southwark, and St. Paul's and Blackfriars. It is dark and alarming under the cavernous arches where the tide rushes fiercely round the piers, gleaming like swift snakes in the dim light. But in all the dark arches are framed a wide space of shining water ahead and the increasing lights of London. And you come out through Blackfriars Bridge at last into a fairyland of light and shadow, water tumbling and sparkling, water ebony and smooth. Round the great curve go the lamps and the lighted trees and the lighted, lumbering trams; and at the end the calm clock of Westminster hangs in the sky.

SIR ALAN HERBERT, *No Boats on the River*, 1932

25

THE WESTERLY WEATHER

THE West Wind reigns over the seas surrounding the coasts of these kingdoms; and from the gateways of the channels, from promontories as if from watch-towers, from estuaries of rivers as if from postern gates, from passage-ways, inlets, straits, firths, the garrison of the Isle and the crews of the ships going and returning look to the westward to judge by the varied splendours of his sunset mantle the mood of that arbitrary ruler. The end of the day is the time to gaze at the kingly face of the Westerly Weather, who is the arbiter of ships' destinies. Benignant and splendid, or splendid and sinister, the western sky reflects the hidden purposes of the royal mind. Clothed in a mantle of dazzling gold or draped in rags of black clouds like a beggar, the might of the Westerly Wind sits enthroned upon the western horizon with the whole North Atlantic as a footstool for his feet and the first twinkling stars making a diadem for his brow.... Some of his sunsets are like pageants devised for the delight of the multitude, when all the gems of the royal treasure-house are displayed above the sea. Others are like the opening of his royal confidence, tinged with thoughts of sadness and compassion in a melancholy splendour meditating upon the short-lived peace of the waters....

He is the war-lord who sends his battalions of Atlantic rollers to the assault of our seaboard. The compelling voice of the West Wind musters up to his service all the might of the ocean. At the bidding of the West Wind there arises a great commotion in the sky above these Islands, and a great rush of waters falls upon our shores. The sky of the Westerly Weather is full of flying clouds, of great big white clouds coming thicker and thicker till they seem to stand welded into a solid canopy, upon whose grey face the lower wrack of the gale, thin, black, and angry-looking, flies past with vertiginous speed.

JOSEPH CONRAD, *The Mirror of the Sea*, 1906

WEATHER FORECAST: **PAINTING** BY JOHN TUNNARD, 1945

STAFFORDSHIRE POTTERY GROUP, c. 1840

THE SAILOR'S RETURN

Oн the times are hard and the wages low,
   Leave her, Johnnie, leave her.
And now ashore again we'll go –
   It's time for us to leave her.

The grub was bad, the voyage long,
   Leave her, Johnnie, leave her,
The seas were high, the gales were strong,
   It's time for us to leave her.

She would not wear, she would not stay,
   Leave her, Johnnie, leave her,
She shipped it green, both night and day,
   It's time for us to leave her.

She would not stay, she would not wear,
   Leave her, Johnnie, leave her.
She shipped it green and she made us swear,
   It's time for us to leave her.

The sails are furled, our work is done,
   Leave her, Johnnie, leave her!
And now ashore we'll take a run –
   It's time for us to leave her.

NINETEENTH-CENTURY
SEA SHANTY

IN THE ORKNEYS

LONG time he lay upon the sunny hill,
  To his father's house below securely bound.
Far off the silent, changing sound was still,
  With the black islands lying thick around.

He saw each separate height, each vaguer hue,
  Where the massed islands rolled in mist away,
And though all ran together in his view
  He knew that unseen straits between them lay.

Often he wondered what new shores were there.
  In thought he saw the still light on the sand,
The shallow water clear in tranquil air,
  And walked through it in joy from strand to strand.

Over the sound a ship so slow would pass
  That in the black hill's gloom it seemed to lie.
The evening sound was smooth like sunken glass,
  And time seemed finished ere the ship passed by.

Grey tiny rocks slept round him where he lay,
  Moveless as they, more still as evening came,
The grasses threw straight shadows far away.
  And from the house his mother called his name.

EDWIN MUIR, 'Childhood'
First Poems, 1925

ON THE SOUTH COAST

No tender-hearted garden crowns,
   No bosomed woods adorn
Our blunt, bow-headed, whale-backed Downs,
   But gnarled and writhen thorn –
Bare slopes where chasing shadows skim,
   And, through the gaps revealed,
Belt upon belt, the wooded, dim
   Blue goodness of the Weald.

Clean of officious fence or hedge,
   Half-wild and wholly tame,
The wise turf cloaks the white cliff edge
   As when the Romans came.
What sign of those that fought and died
   At shift of sword and sword?
The barrow and the camp abide,
   The sunlight and the sward.

Here leaps ashore the full Sou'west
   All heavy-winged with brine,
Here lies above the folded crest
   The Channel's leaden line;
And here the sea-fogs lap and cling,
   And here, each warning each,
The sheep-bells and the ship-bells ring
   Along the hidden beach.

RUDYARD KIPLING, from 'Sussex'
The Five Nations, 1903

THE LAND OF LITTLE HARBOURS

AND the winter went, and many other winters,
And we walked by the sea's edge to Cornelian bay,
By a shore of wreckage, of the sundered timbers,
Finding dark jet and the wonders of the ammonite;
All there was of men was the smoke above their houses
Below the green baize cliff, up to the ruined castle,
Giving on the harbour, on the masted shipping.
So was all their coast, to Whitby and beyond,
A land of little harbours, little stilt-like houses
Standing in the tides;
Sometimes a doorway of the jawbones of a whale,
A netted anchor, or the figure from a ship,
Dredged from the seas, stood in a white-washed yard
For spoil from the shoals, from shimmer of the mackerel;
And the year went in wonders, the great spring-tide
Ebbed with the moon, in an electric morning
When air sparked and flashed, when all the world was new;
That tide left the harbour dry; the keel-less ships
Leaned to one side, toppling on the sand;
It ebbed at another shore, far down the sea,
Laid bare for this, refulgent with new light
On rocks, not seen before, new islands in the plain
Glittering with pools, the little fronded seas
Where waved green weeds or dried their greener tresses
On mermaid rocks and crackled in their pods,
Instinct with iodine. The archipelago
Glistened, all shining, new-risen from the sea;
The salt airs out upon those frontiers
Were the breath of Creation till the spring-tide flowed

When the isles sank and vanished, and the leaning vessels
Righted their keels: the high tide, towering
Took new sands and piled against the piers
Swollen in fury, as in a race of waters,
All, all for nothing, for one morning of the spring.
At another season, to a dawn of mist,
The bay was a blue gulf, the millpond ocean
Made no sound but slept against the cliffs,
As in a slumbering crater; the long lights shone in it
Like shadows upon oil, if oil lay on the water
And a cloud of smoke above it; till the lifting day
Of late August morning showed the herring-fleet
Come back from the Dogger Bank with brown sails furled
Like a huge Armada filling all the bay;
The shore was all stalls, the herring-silver,
Shoal of many millions, gutted, put in salt,
Peopled the barrels from the emptied seas
That jangled with that silver, leaping in the nets
Through the moonlit night, now massacred and dead;
All day the herring-fleet, a town of tents,
Kept the blue plain, Tartarian wide,
But, at night, struck camp and sailed into the dawn
To set up their town upon the shallow seas
For the shoal of herring, a shadow on the water
A shade, like smoke, upon it, hiding the green sand. . . .

SACHEVERELL SITWELL
from 'Upon an Image from Dante'
Canons of Giant Art, 1933

EAST ANGLIAN BATHE

OH when the early morning at the seaside
　　Took us with hurrying steps from Horsey Mere
To see the whistling bent-grass on the leeside
　　And then the tumbled breaker-line appear,
On high, the clouds with mighty adumbration
　　Sailed over us to seaward fast and clear
And jellyfish in quivering isolation
　　Lay silted in the dry sand of the breeze
And we, along the table-land of beach blown
　　Went gooseflesh from our shoulders to our knees
And ran to catch the football, each to each thrown,
　　In the soft and swirling music of the seas.

There splashed about our ankles as we waded
　　Those intersecting wavelets morning-cold,
And sudden dark a patch of sea was shaded,
　　And sudden light, another patch would hold
The warmth of whirling atoms in a sun-shot
　　And underwater sandstorm green and gold.
So in we dived and louder than a gunshot
　　Sea-water broke in fountains down the ear.
How cold the swim, how chattering cold the drying,
　　How welcoming the inland reeds appear,
The wood-smoke and the breakfast and the frying,
　　And your warm freshwater ripples, Horsey Mere.

JOHN BETJEMAN
New Bats in Old Belfries, 1945

BANK HOLIDAY

THERE was cricket on the sand, and sand in the sponge cake, sand-flies in the watercress, and foolish, mulish, religious donkeys on the unwilling trot. Girls undressed in slipping tents of propriety; under invisible umbrellas, stout ladies dressed for the male and immoral sea. Little naked navvies dug canals; children with spades and no ambition built fleeting castles; wispy young men, outside the bathing-huts, whistled at substantial young women and dogs who desired thrown stones more than the bones of elephants. Recalcitrant uncles huddled over luke ale in the tiger-striped marquees. Mothers in black, like wobbling mountains, gasped under the discarded dresses of daughters who shrilly braved the goblin waves. And fathers, in the once-a-year sun, took fifty winks. Oh, think of all the fifty winks along the paper-bagged sand.

Liquorice allsorts, and Welsh hearts, were melting, and the sticks of rock, that we all sucked, were like barbers' poles made of rhubarb.

In the distance, surrounded by disappointed theoreticians and an ironmonger with a drum, a cross man on an orange-box shouted that holidays were wrong.

And the waves rolled in, with rubber ducks and clerks upon them.

I remember the patient, laborious, and enamouring hobby, or profession, of burying relatives in sand.

I remember the princely pastime of pouring sand, from cupped hands or buckets, down collars and tops of dresses; the shriek, the shake, the slap.

I can remember the boy by himself, the beachcombing lone-wolf, hungrily waiting at the edge of family cricket; the friendless fielder, the boy uninvited to bat or to tea.

I remember the smell of sea and seaweed, wet flesh, wet hair, wet bathing-dresses, the warm smell as of a rabbity field after rain, the

35

smell of pop and splashed sunshades and toffee, the stable-and-straw smell of hot, tossed, tumbled, dug, and trodden sand, the swill-and-gas-lamp smell of Saturday night, though the sun shone strong, from the bellying beer-tents, the smell of the vinegar on shelled cockles, winkle-smell, shrimp-smell, the dripping-oily backstreetwinter-smell of chips in newspapers, the smell of ships from the sun-dazed docks round the corner of the sand-hills, the smell of the known and paddled-in sea moving, full of the drowned and herrings, out and away and beyond and further still towards the antipodes that hung their koala-bears and Maoris, kangaroos, and boomerangs, upside down over the backs of the stars.

And the noise of pummelling Punch, and Judy falling, and a clock tolling or telling no time in the tenantless town; now and again a bell from a lost tower or a train on the lines behind us clearing its throat, and always the hopeless, ravenous swearing and pleading of the gulls, donkey-bray and hawker-cry, harmonicas and toy trumpets, shouting and laughing and singing, hooting of tugs and tramps, the clip of the chair-attendant's puncher, the motor-boat coughing in the bay, and the same hymn and washing of the sea that was heard in the Bible.

'If it could only just, if it could only just' your lips said again and again as you scooped, in the hob-hot sand, dungeons, garages, torture-chambers, train tunnels, arsenals, hangars for zeppelins, witches' kitchens, vampires' parlours, smugglers' cellars, trolls' grog-shops, sewers, under a ponderous and cracking castle, 'If it could only just be like this for ever and ever amen.'

DYLAN THOMAS, *Quite Early one Morning*, 1954

OUTHEND (DETAIL): WATERCOLOUR DRAWING BY EDWARD ARDIZZONE, 1955

THE PIER HEAD, WALBERSWICK: PAINTING BY PHILIP WILSON STEER, R.A., 1888

SUMMER BEACH

For how long known this boundless wash of light,
   This smell of purity, this gleaming waste,
This wind? This brown, strewn wrack how old a sight,
   These pebbles round to touch and salt to taste.

See, the slow marbled heave, the liquid arch,
   Before the waves' procession to the land
Flowers in foam; the ripples' onward march,
   Their last caresses on the pure hard sand.

For how long known these bleaching corks, new-made
   Smooth and enchanted from the lapping sea?
Since first I laboured with a wooden spade
   Against this background of Eternity.

FRANCES CORNFORD
Travelling Home, 1948

BRIGHTON

AT night the Front like coloured barley-sugar; but now
Soft blue, all soda, the air goes flat over flower-beds,
Blue railings and beaches; below, half-painted boats, bow
Up, settle in sand, names like Moss-Rose and Dolphin
Drying in a breeze that flicks at the ribs of the tide.
The chalk coastline folds up its wings of Beachy Head
And Worthing, fluttering white over water like brides.
Regency squares, the Pavilion, oysters and mussels and gin. . . .

Sussex *v*. Lancashire, the air birded and green after rain,
Dew on syringa and cherry. Seaward the water
Is satin, pale emerald, fretted with lace at the edges,
The whole sky rinsed easy like nerves after pain.
May here is childhood, lost somewhere between and never
Recovered, but again moved nearer, as a lever
Turned on the pier flickers the Past into pictures.
A time of immediacy, optimism, without stricture.

Postcards and bathing-machines and old prints.
Something comes back, the inkling, the momentary hint
Of what we had wanted to be, though differently now,
For the conditions are different and what we had wanted
We wanted as we were then, without conscience, unhaunted,
And given the chance must refuse to want it again.
Only, occasionally, we escape, we return where we were:
Watching cricket at Brighton, Cornford bowling through
   sea-scented air.

ALAN ROSS, *Something of the Sea*, 1954

BESIDE THE BAY

He stood, a worn-out City clerk –
  Who'd toiled, and seen no holiday,
For forty years from dawn to dark –
  Alone beside Caermarthen Bay.

He felt the salt spray on his lips;
  Heard children's voices on the sands;
Up the sun's path he saw the ships
  Sail on and on to other lands;

And laughed aloud. Each sight and sound
  To him was joy too deep for tears;
He sat him on the beach, and bound
  A blue bandana round his ears;

And thought how, posted near his door,
  His own green door on Camden Hill,
Two bands at least, most likely more,
  Were mingling at their own sweet will

Verdi with Vance. And at the thought
  He laughed again, and softly drew
That *Morning Herald* that he'd bought
  Forth from his breast, and read it through.

C. S. CALVERLEY
Fly Leaves, 1872

LANDSCAPE

No lovelier hills than thine have laid
  My tired thoughts to rest:
No peace of lovelier valleys made
  Like peace within my breast.

Thine are the woods whereto my soul,
  Out of the noontide beam,
Flees for a refuge green and cool
  And tranquil as a dream.

Thy breaking seas like trumpets peal;
  Thy clouds – how oft have I
Watched their bright towers of silence steal
  Into infinity!

My heart within me faints to roam
  In thought even far from thee:
Thine be the grave whereto I come,
  And thine my darkness be.

WALTER DE LA MARE, 'England'
Poems, 1906

THE DEVIL'S ELBOW, ROKEBY: WATERCOLOUR DRAWING BY J. S. COTMAN, *c.* 1807

THE BRIGHT CLOUD: DRAWING BY SAMUEL PALMER, *c.* 1831

THE EVERLASTING HILLS

I STOOD at the foot of Rocky Carradon:
The massive monuments of a vast religion,
Piled by the strength of unknown hands, were there;
The everlasting hills, around, afar,
Uplifted their huge fronts, the natural altars
Reared by the Earth to the surrounding God.
I heard a Voice, as the sound of many waters: –
'What do'st thou here, Elijah?' And I said,
'What doth he here, Man that is born of woman?
The clouds may haunt these mountains; the fierce storm
Coiled in his caverned lair – that wild torrent
Leaps from a native land: but Man! O Lord!
What doth he here!'

REV. ROBERT STEPHEN HAWKER
from 'A Rapture on the Cornish Hills'
Records of the Western Shore, 1832

THE FIELDS OF AMARANTH

Very old are the woods;
   And the buds that break
Out of the brier's boughs,
   When March winds wake,
So old with their beauty are –
   Oh, no man knows
Through what wild centuries
   Roves back the rose.

Very old are the brooks;
   And the rills that rise
Where snow sleeps cold beneath
   The azure skies
Sing such a history
   Of come and gone,
Their every drop is as wise
   As Solomon.

Very old are we men;
   Our dreams are tales
Told in dim Eden
   By Eve's nightingales;
We wake and whisper awhile,
   But, the day gone by
Silence and sleep like fields
   Of amaranth lie.

WALTER DE LA MARE, ' All That's Past'
The Listeners, 1914

ENGLISH PASTURAGE

THE moss-grey mansion of my father stands
Park'd in an English pasturage as fair
As any that the grass-green isle can show.
Above it rise deep-wooded lawns; below
A brook runs riot thro' the pleasant lands,
And blabs its secrets to the merry air.
The village peeps from out deep poplars, where
A grey bridge spans the stream; and all beyond,
In sloping vales and sweet acclivities,
The many-dimpled, laughing landscape lies. . . .

JULIAN FANE, 'Apethorpe'
in *Julian Fane, A Memoir*
by Robert Lytton, 1871

THE ROOFLESS PAST

WHAT is Stonehenge? It is the roofless past;
Man's ruinous myth; his uninterred adoring
Of the unknown in sunrise cold and red;
His quest of stars that arch his doomed exploring.

And what is Time but shadows that were cast
By these storm-sculptured stones while centuries fled?
The stones remain; their stillness can outlast
The skies of history hurrying overhead.

SIEGFRIED SASSOON, *The Heart's Journey*, 1928

STONEHENGE: DIAMOND-POINT ENGRAVING ON GLASS BY LAURENCE WHISTLER, 1955

BOLSOVER CASTLE: WATERCOLOUR DRAWING BY JOHN PIPER, 1944

THE PLEASURES OF DECAY

BLESS'D is the man in whose sequester'd glade
Some ancient abbey's walls diffuse their shade,
With mould'ring windows pierc'd, and turrets crown'd,
And pinnacles with clinging ivy bound.
Bless'd too is he, who, 'midst his tufted trees,
Some ruin'd castle's lofty towers sees,
Imbosom'd high upon the mountain's brow,
Or nodding o'er the stream that glides below.
Nor yet unenvy'd, to whose humbler lot
Falls the retir'd and antiquated cot,
Its roof with weeds and mosses cover'd o'er,
And honeysuckles climbing round the door,
While mantling vines along its walls are spread
And clust'ring ivy decks the chimney's head.
Still happier he (if conscious of his prize)
Who sees some temple's broken columns rise
'Midst sculptur'd fragments, shiver'd by their fall,
And tott'ring remnants of its marble wall;
Where ev'ry beauty of correct design,
And vary'd elegance of art, combine
With nature's softest tints, matur'd by time
And the warm influence of a genial clime.

RICHARD PAYNE KNIGHT
The Landscape, 1794

51

ENGLISH CHARACTER

How stately stand yon pines upon the hill,
How soft the murmurs of that living rill,
And o'er the park's tall paling, scarcely higher,
Peeps the low Church and shows the modest spire,
Unnumber'd violets on those banks appear,
And all the first-born beauties of the year.
The grey-green blossoms of the willow bring
The large wild bees upon the labouring wing.
Then comes the Summer with augmented pride,
Whose pure small streams along the valleys glide:
Her richer Flora their brief charms display;
And, as the fruit advances, fall away.
Then shall th'autumnal yellow clothe the leaf,
What time the reaper binds the burden'd sheaf:
Then silent groves denote the dying year,
The morning frost, and noon-tide gossamer;
And all be silent in the scene around,
All save the distant sea's uncertain sound,
Or here and there the gun whose loud report
Proclaims to man that Death is but his sport;
And then the wintry winds begin to blow,
Then fall the flaky stars of gathering snow,
When on the thorn the ripening sloe, yet blue,
Takes the bright varnish of the morning dew;
The aged moss grows brittle on the pale,
The dry boughs splinter in the windy gale,
And every changing season of the year
Stamps on the scene its English character.

REV. GEORGE CRABBE, *Poetical Works*, 1834

THE ENGLISH IDEAL

In some small hamlet on the lonely plain,
Where Thames, thro' meadows, rolls his mazy train;
Or where high Windsor, thick with greens array'd,
Waves his old oaks, and spreads his ample shade,
Fancy has figur'd out our calm retreat;
Already round the visionary seat
Our limes begin to shoot, our flow'rs to spring,
The brooks to murmur, and the birds to sing.
Where dost thou lie, thou thinly-peopled green?
Thou nameless lawn, and village yet unseen?
Where sons, contented with their native ground,
Ne'er travell'd further than ten furlongs round;
And the tann'd peasant, and his ruddy bride,
Were born together, and together died.
Where early larks best tell the morning-light,
And only Philomel disturbs the night,
'Midst gardens here my humble pile shall rise,
With sweets surrounded of ten thousand dyes;
All savage where th'embroider'd gardens end,
The haunt of echoes shall my woods ascend;
And O! if heav'n th'ambitious thought approve,
A rill shall warble cross the gloomy grove,
A little rill, o'er pebbly beds convey'd,
Gush down the steep, and glitter thro' the glade.
What cheering scents those bord'ring banks exhale!
How loud that heifer lows from yonder vale!

THOMAS TICKELL, from 'To a Lady before Marriage'
Poems, 1790 (written *c.* 1720)

COTTAGES IN THE AIR

THESE humble dwellings remind the contemplative spectator of a production of Nature, and may (using a strong expression) rather be said to have grown than to have been erected; – to have risen, by an instinct of their own, out of the native rock – so little is there in them of formality, such is their wildness and beauty. Among the numerous recesses and projections in the walls and in the different stages of their roofs, are seen bold and harmonious effects of contrasted sunshine and shadow. . . . Nor will the singular beauty of the chimneys escape the eye of the attentive traveller. Sometimes a low chimney, almost upon a level with the roof, is overlaid with a slate, supported upon four slender pillars, to prevent the wind from driving the smoke down the chimney. Others are of a quadrangular shape, rising one or two feet above the roof: which low square is often surmounted by a tall cylinder, giving to the cottage chimney the most beautiful shape in which it is ever seen. Nor will it be too fanciful or refined to remark that there is a pleasing harmony between a tall chimney of this circular form and the living column of smoke, through the still air ascending from it. These dwellings, mostly built, as has been said, of rough unhewn stone, are roofed with slates, which were rudely taken from the quarry before the present art of splitting them was understood, and are, therefore, rough and uneven in their surface, so that both the coverings and sides of the houses have furnished places of rest for the seeds of lichens, mosses, ferns, and flowers. Hence buildings, which in their very form call to mind the processes of Nature, do thus, clothed with this vegetable garb, appear to be received into the bosom of the living principle of things, as it acts and exists among the woods and fields . . . ;

WILLIAM WORDSWORTH
A Description of the Scenery of the Lakes, 1822

CASTLES ON THE GROUND

EWBANK'D inside and Atco'd out, the English suburban residence and the garden which is an integral part of it stand trim and lovingly cared for in the mild sunshine. Everything is in its place. The abruptness, the barbarities of the world, are far away. There is not much sound, except perhaps the musical whirr and clack of a mowing machine being pushed back and forth over a neighbouring lawn and the clink of cups and saucers and a soft footfall as tea is got ready indoors. There is not much movement either: a wire-haired terrier lazily trotting round the garden in a not very hopeful search for something new to smell, and the pages of a newspaper being turned and refolded by some leisurely individual in a deck chair. It is an almost windless day. The leaves of the virginia creeper (*ampelopsis veitchii*) which climbs the rough-cast wall just beside the window of the best bedroom hardly stir, and even the birds only hop – and flutter a few feet in the air, and hop again – along the ornamental ridge of the red-tiled roof.

Perhaps a tradesman's van is making its rounds. Perhaps at this moment, on the other side of the screen of privet hedge and may and laburnum which separates the garden scent of new grass cuttings from the warm peppery scent that radiates from asphalt pavements in summer-time, the baker's boy is halting his cart. In another moment he will push open the low wooden gate with its embossed copper name-plate on the rail, and will carelessly let it swing to behind him as he strides up the gravel path with his basket of loaves on his arm. But this is only the tradesman's entrance, and the faint squeak of the hinge and the sound the latch makes as the gate swings back will not be very disturbing; nor will his footsteps as he passes behind the green-painted trellis with the rockery at its foot towards the kitchen door at the side of the house. . . .

For different Englishmen, of course, the picture varies in detail –
but not very much. We have described the day-dream of the
Englishman who belongs to one of the more prosperous suburbs –
Cheam, perhaps, or Rickmansworth or Mill Hill – and to the class
that wears a linen collar to go to work in, but we could just as easily
have chosen an Englishman a little lower in the social scale and
described his ideal villa instead, set but a short way back from the
bustle of some arterial road in Osterley or the outskirts of Birmingham. This one has but a modest lawn in front, perhaps with a cast
stone bird-bath, and a wooden paling instead of a hedge of luxuriant
flowering shrubs and trees; but this, it should be said, is chiefly
because it is so much newer. There may only be a number on the
gate, on a small oval china plate, instead of a name. Instead of the
pillared or half-timbered porch there is a simpler brick arch beneath
a plain tiled gable, and instead of the rack full of walking sticks in the
hall a china umbrella stand.

Alternatively, we could have looked a little higher in the social
scale and set the house in its own grounds at the centre of a circular
gravel drive bordered with rhododendrons and variegated laurel and
other shrubs. We would then have mentioned the scent of Surrey
pines and the fact that the front hall contains a polished table with a
china bowl on it full of visiting cards. Beyond this hall we would
have noted a larger lounge hall with oak-panelled walls instead of
wallpaper or lincrusta, and at the end of it an open-well staircase with
polished treads, lighted by its own round-topped window. This, as
in the other houses, is leaded into rectangular panes, but it has a stout
oak transom and a small inset of coloured heraldic glass. In the hall,
in addition to the faint smell of furniture polish, we would have
noted an even fainter scent of Pears' soap coming from the down-
stairs cloakroom.

J. M. RICHARDS, *The Castles on the Ground*, 1946

HOME

I STOOD upon a lawn whose greensward lay
Smooth-levell'd by the scythe; two mulberry trees
Beyond it stretch'd their old and foliaged arms;
Th' acacia quiver'd in the wind: the thick
And deep-leaved laurel darken'd the recess
Of massive buttresses; the mansion's walls,
Grey in antiquity, were tapestried o'er
With the fig's downy leaves, and roses climb'd
Clust'ring around the casements' gothic panes.
With terraces and verdant slopes, where pines
Arch'd their plumed boughs, and fruits espalier-train'd
Were mix'd with myrtles and with arbute-trees,
The scene behind look'd sylvan: higher rose
The bounding hill, whose turfy paths were track'd
Up the bare herbage, gnarl'd with scatter'd crags
And topt with straggling firs or chestnuts broad;
A sweet yet solemn landscape, for it spoke
Of sacred home. . . .

SIR CHARLES ABRAHAM ELTON
The Brothers, 1820

AN ENGLISH ARTIST

THIS is the vale he knew –
Its games of sun and shower,
Willow and breeze, the truant
Here-and-there of the Stour,
And an immutable church tower
To polarize the view.

Yet, earnestly though we look
At such hard facts, the mill,
The lucid tower and the lock
Are something less than real.
For this was never the vale
He saw, and showed unique –

A landscape of the heart,
Of passion nursed on calm,
Where cloud and stream drew out
His moods, and love became
A brush in his hand, and the elm tree
Lived like a stroke of art.

His sunburst inspiration
Made earthly forms so true
To life, so new to vision,
That now the actual view
Seems a mere phantom, through
Whose blur we glimpse creation. . . .

CECIL DAY LEWIS, from 'Dedham Vale'
in *Time and Tide*, December 25, 1954

N THE STOUR, DEDHAM CHURCH IN THE DISTANCE: PAINTING BY JOHN CONSTABLE, R.A., *c.* 1810

WEDGWOOD POTTERY: THE RUSSIAN IMPERIAL DINNER SERVICE, 1774, PAINTED WITH ENGLISH LANDSCA

THE ENGLISH ART

To improve the scenery of a country, and to display its native beauties with advantage, is an ART which originated in England, and has therefore been called *English Gardening*; yet as this expression is not sufficiently appropriate, especially since Gardening, in its more confined sense of *Horticulture*, has been likewise brought to the greatest perfection in this country, I have adopted the term *Landscape Gardening*, as most proper, because the art can only be advanced and perfected by the united powers of the *landscape painter* and the *practical gardener*. The former must conceive a plan, which the latter may be able to execute; for though the painter may represent a beautiful landscape on his canvas, and even surpass Nature by the combination of her choicest materials, yet the luxuriant imagination of the *painter* must be subjected to the *gardener's* practical knowledge in planting, digging, and moving earth; that the simplest and readiest means of accomplishing each design may be suggested; since it is not by vast labour, or great expense, that Nature is generally to be improved.

HUMPHRY REPTON
Sketches and Hints on Landscape Gardening, 1795

THE house, though low in the park, is yet above the adjacent country, which it overlooks to a very distant horizon: it is surrounded by a lawn, of fine uneven ground, and diversified with large clumps, little groups, and single trees; it is open in front, but covered on one side by the Witchberry hills; on the other side, and behind, by the eminences in the park, which are high and steep, and all overspread with a lofty hanging wood. The lawn pressing to the foot, or creeping up the slopes of these hills, and sometimes winding along glades into the depth of the wood, traces a beautiful outline to a sylvan scene, already rich to luxuriance in massiness of foliage, and stateliness of growth.

But though the wood appears to be entire, it in reality opens frequently into lawns, which occupy much of the space within it: in the number, the variety, and the beauty of these lawns, in the shades of the separations between them, in their beauties also, and their varieties, the glory of Hagley consists. . . .

An octagon seat, sacred to the memory of Thomson, and erected on his favourite spot, stands on the brow of a steep; a mead winds along the valley beneath, till it is lost on either hand between some trees; opposite to the seat, a noble wood crowns the top, and feathers down to the bottom, of a large, oval, swelling hill; as it descends on one side, the distant country becomes the offskip; over the fall on the other side the Clent hills appear; a dusky antique tower stands just below them, at the extremity of the wood; and in the midst of it is seen a Doric portico, called Pope's Building, with part of the lawn before it; the scene is very simple; the principle features are great; they prevail over all the rest, and are intimately connected. . . .

In an obscure corner, and shut out from all view, is a hermitage, composed of roots and of moss; high banks, and a thick covert darkened with horse-chestnuts, confine the sequestered spot; a little rill trickles through it, and two small pieces of water occupy the bottom; they are seen on one side through groups of trees; the other is open, but covered with fern; this valley is the extremity of the park, and the Clent hills rise in all their irregularity immediately above it. . . .

No strong lines are drawn; no striking objects are admitted; but all is of an even temper, all mild, placid, and serene, in the gayest season of the day not more than cheerful, in the stillest watch of night not gloomy; the scene is indeed peculiarly adapted to the tranquillity of the latter, when the moon seems to repose her light on the thick foliage of the grove, and steadily marks the shade of every bough; it is delightful then to saunter here, and see the grass, and the gossamer which entwines it, glistening with dew; to listen and hear nothing stir, except perhaps a withered leaf dropping gently through a tree; and sheltered from the chill, to catch the freshness of the evening air; a solitary urn, chosen by Mr. Pope for the spot, and now inscribed to his memory, when shewn by a gleam of moonlight through the trees, fixes that thoughtfulness and composure, to which the mind is insensibly led by the rest of this elegant scene.

T. WHATELY, *Observations on Modern Gardening*, 1770

BUT see the fading many-coloured woods,
Shade deepening over shade, the country round
Imbrown; a crowded umbrage, dusk and dun,
Of every hue, from wan declining green
To sooty dark. These now the lonesome Muse,
Low-whispering, lead into their leaf-strown walks,
And give the season in its latest view.

JAMES THOMSON, *The Seasons*, 1730

THE PICTURESQUE

Now I gain the mountain's brow
What a landskip lies below!
No clouds, no vapours intervene,
But the gay, the open scene
Does the face of Nature show
In all the hues of Heaven's bow!
And, swelling to embrace the light,
Spreads around beneath the sight.

   Old castles on the cliffs arise,
Proudly towering in the skies!
Rushing from the woods, the spires
Seem from hence ascending fires!
Half his beams Apollo sheds
On the yellow mountain-heads!
Gilds the fleeces of the flocks:
And glitters on the broken rocks!

   Below me trees unnumbered rise,
Beautiful in various dyes:
The gloomy pine, the poplar blue,
The yellow beech, the sable yew,
The slender fir that taper grows,
The sturdy oak with broad-spread boughs.
And beyond, the purple grove,
Haunt of Phillis, queen of love!
Gaudy as the opening dawn,
Lies a long and level lawn,
On which a dark hill, steep and high,
Holds and charms the wandering eye!
Deep are his feet in Towy's flood,

His sides are clothed with waving wood,
And ancient towers crown his brow,
That cast an aweful look below;
Whose ragged walls the ivy creeps,
And with her arms from falling keeps;
So both a safety from the wind
On mutual dependence find.

    'Tis now the raven's bleak abode;
'Tis now th'apartment of the toad;
And there the fox securely feeds;
And there the poisonous adder breeds
Concealed in ruins, moss and weeds;
While, ever and anon, there falls
Huge heaps of hoary mouldered walls . . .

    Ever charming, ever new,
When will the landskip tire the view!
The fountain's fall, the river's flow,
The woody valleys, warm and low;
The windy summit, wild and high,
Roughly rushing on the sky!
The pleasant seat, the ruined tower,
The naked rock, the shady bower;
The town and village, dome and farm,
Each give each a double charm,
As pearls upon an Aethiop's arm.

REV. JOHN DYER, from 'Grongar Hill,'
in *Miscellaneous Poems by Several Hands,* 1726

IN THE FRUITFUL FLAT LAND

THE train. A hot July. On either hand
Our sober, fruitful, unemphatic land,
This Cambridge country plain beneath the sky
Where I was born, and grew, and hope to die.

Look! where the willows hide a rushy pool,
And the old horse goes squelching down to cool,
One angler's rod against their silvery green,
Still seen today as once by Bewick seen.

A cottage there, thatched sadly, like its earth,
Where crimson ramblers make a shortlived mirth;
Here, only flies the flick-tail cows disturb
Among the shaven meads and willow-herb.

There, rounded hay-ricks solemn in the yard,
Barns gravely, puritanically tarred,
Next heavy elms that guard the ripening grain
And fields, and elms, and corn, and fields again.

Over the soft savannahs of the corn,
Like ships the hot white butterflies are borne,
While clouds pass slowly on the flower-blue dome
Like spirits in a vast and peaceful home.

Over the Dyke I watch their shadows flow
As the Icenian watched them long ago;
So let me in this Cambridge calm July
Fruitfully live and undistinguished die.

FRANCES CORNFORD, *Travelling Home*, 1948

AMID THE BARREN HILLS

THERE is a spot, 'mid barren hills,
   Where winter howls, and driving rain;
But, if the dreary tempest chills,
   There is a light that warms again.

The house is old, the trees are bare,
   Moonless above bends twilight's dome;
But what on earth is half so dear –
   So longed for – as the hearth of home?

The mute bird sitting on the stone,
   The dank moss dripping from the wall,
The thorn-trees gaunt, the walks o'ergrown,
   I love them – how I love them all! . . .

A little and a lone green lane
   That opened on a common wide;
A distant, dreamy, dim blue chain
   Of mountains, circling every side.

A heaven so clear, an earth so calm,
   So sweet, so soft, so hushed an air;
And, deepening still the dream-like charm,
   Wild moor-sheep feeding everywhere.

EMILY BRONTË, from 'A Little While'
Wuthering Heights, etc., 1850

TWEED

THREE crests against the saffron sky,
  Beyond the purple plain,
The kind remembered melody
  Of Tweed once more again.

Wan water from the border hills,
  Dear voice from the old years,
Thy distant music lulls and stills,
  And moves to quiet tears.

Like a loved ghost thy fabled flood
  Fleets through the dusky land;
Where Scott, come home to die, has stood,
  My feet returning stand.

A mist of memory broods and floats,
  The Border waters flow;
The air is full of ballad notes,
  Borne out of long ago.

Old songs that sung themselves to me,
  Sweet through a boy's day-dream,
While trout below the blossom'd tree
  Plashed in the golden stream.

Twilight, and Tweed, and Eildon Hill,
  Fair and too fair you be;
You tell me that the voice is still
  That should have welcomed me.

ANDREW LANG, *Grass of Parnassus*, 1892

THAMES

I SEE the winding water make
A short and then a shorter lake
  As here stand I,
  And house-boat high,
Survey the Upper Thames.
  By sun the mud is amber-dyed
  In ripples slow and flat and wide,
  That flap against the house-boat side
And flop away in gems.

In mud and elder-scented shade
A reach away the breach is made
  By dive and shout
  That circles out
To Henley tower and town;
  And 'Boats for Hire' the rafters ring,
  And pink on white the roses cling,
  And red the bright geraniums swing
In baskets dangling down.

When shall I see the Thames again?
The prow-promoted gems again,
  As beefy ATS
  Without their hats
Coming shooting through the bridge?
  And 'cheerioh' and 'cheeri-bye'
  Across the waste of waters die,
  And low the mists of evening lie
And lightly skims the midge.

JOHN BETJEMAN
New Bats in Old Belfries, 1945

EVENING IN DORSET

SWEET Be'mi'ster, that bist a-bound,
By green an' woody hills all round,
Wi' hedges, reachen up between
A thousand vields o' zummer green,
Where elems' lofty heads do drow
Their sheades vor hay-meakers below,
An' wild hedge-flow'rs do charm the souls
O' maidens in their evenen strolls.

When I o' Zunday nights with Jeane
Do saunter drough a vield or leane,
Where elder blossoms be a-spread
Above the eltrot's milk-white head,
An' flow'rs o' blackberries do blow
Upon the brembles, white as snow,
To be outdone avore my zight
By Jean's gay frock o' dazzlen white;

Oh! then there's nothen that's 'ithout
Thy hills that I do ho about, –
Noo bigger pleace, noo gayer town,
Beyond thy sweet bells' dyen soun',
As they do ring, or strike the hour,
At evenen vrom thy wold red tow'r.
No; shelter still my head, an' keep
My bwones when I do vall asleep.

WILLIAM BARNES
Poems of Rural Life in the Dorset Dialect, 1844
(revised text 1861)

EVENING AT SELBORNE

WHEN day declining sheds a milder gleam,
What time the may-fly haunts the pool or stream;
When the still owl skims round the grassy mead,
What time the timorous hare limps forth to feed;
Then be the time to steal adown the vale,
And listen to the vagrant cuckoo's tale;
To hear the clamorous curlew call his mate,
Or the soft quail his tender pain relate;
To see the swallow sweep the darkening plain
Belated, to support her infant train . . .
   While deepening shades obscure the face of day
To yonder bench leaf-sheltered let us stray,
Till blended objects fail the swimming sight,
And all the fading landscape sinks in night;
To hear the drowsy dor come brushing by
With buzzing wing, or the shrill cricket cry;
To see the feeding bat glance through the wood;
To catch the distant falling of the flood;
While o'er the cliff the awakened churn-owl hung
Through the still gloom protracts his chattering song;
While high in air, and poised upon his wings,
Unseen, the soft enamoured wood-lark sings: . . .
   Each rural sight, each sound, each smell, combine;
The tinkling sheep-bell, or the breath of kine;
The new-mown hay that scents the swelling breeze,
Or cottage-chimney smoking through the trees. . . .

REV. GILBERT WHITE
The Natural History of Selborne, 1789

71

ABBEY BY MOONLIGHT

It was evening when I stepped ashore by the old Anchor Inn at Tintern, the evening of the harvest moon. On that night, in less prosaic times, lovers came from far and near to whisper promises to each other while, from the west end of the abbey, they watched the full moon fill the great empty circle in the head of the eastern window.

The building was glowing in the evening light, warm as the rose-tinted walls of Petra. After sunset a shimmering veil of mist filled the valley, through which the church appeared tenuous and un-substantial.

I wandered among the idle pillars and arches while the evening lost its light. Dew began to fall. Owls called from wood to wood 'Oo, ooloo oo. Oo ooloo oo.' It grew darker. A pig grunted; a calf bellowed. Still darker. A woman and a man palavered on the road. Dark cars rushed past in the darkness. 'Oo, ooloo ooloo oo.'

Then over the high, wooded, eastern hill came the moon, golden in the deep indigo sky. Steadily it grew from a shallow crescent to a fuller arc, then to a half circle, to three-quarters, to the full sphere of light. I was alone, and had no wish for whispers from any one. From the southern meadow I watched the shadows creep into the aisles, and the transepts emerge from dark shapes of their own creating.

As the mist cleared away, the church stood revealed in the moon-light, so calm, so still, yet no calmer than the bones of those who lie beneath its turf; priests, deacons, laymen, all who, in their own way, have swelled the universal song of praise. Some of us worship life because we fear death, some of us worship death because we fear life. There is room for us all. Jackdaws now praise God where once the white-robed monks sang hymns.

ROBERT GIBBINGS, *Coming Down the Wye*, 1942

TINTERN ABBEY: WATERCOLOUR DRAWING BY THOMAS GIRTIN

NOSTELL PRIORY: EIGHTEENTH-CENTURY DOLL'S HOUSE

THE ENGLISH STYLE

ABOVE all else the English scene is artificial. No race has talked about Nature or drawn inspiration from her to the extent that we have, and nowhere in the world is she kept more firmly under control than in England. Our landscape, of which we are justly proud, is a work of art in the exact meaning of the term: save in a few isolated pockets in the Fells or on Dartmoor, no acre of the English countryside is, nor has been for centuries, in anything that approaches a natural state. . . .

The role of architect and town planner here has, therefore, for a long time, at least since the seventeenth century, been subtly different from that of his colleagues abroad. The relation between architecture and landscape is far closer and more complicated where the latter can be made to conform to the prevailing taste almost as easily as bricks and mortar. . . . Not only did the canons of architectural taste materially alter the appearance of the landscape, but the character of the landscape insensibly affected the canons of architectural taste. And this it is which gives to English architecture its unique quality. Versailles and Caserta spread the influence of their pompous formality over hundreds of acres of the surrounding countryside; but in the country houses of England, with certain notable exceptions (such as Blenheim and Seaton Delaval, which, noble works as they are, retain a faint exoticism that is understandable in a Leoni but puzzling in a Vanbrugh), the formality has been softened, the pediments and porticoes rendered less rigid, and the fluttering and writhing of the draperies pendant from the statues along the balustrade are stirred by a more tempered, less violent, wind than that which blows down the long colonnades of the high Baroque: for, thanks to the modifying influence of the landscape, the grand gesture, the theatrical sweep, are here made to appear, ever so faintly, absurd.

OSBERT LANCASTER, in *This Britain*, 1951

CLASSIC GROUND

APPROACH we then this classic ground;
More gentle name was never found
By chance, nor more of picturing sound
    To tell the spirit of the scene;
Be Dovedale ours this April day,
This April day that sheen or gray
May whip the wavelets into spray
    Or flood with sun the margent green.

For all that wild work on the height
And driven clouds hailstone-gray, and fight
Of venturers on the ridge, delight
    Is April's way and Dovedale's mind;
These chasms and spikes that might elsewhere
Be monsters, horror's host, despair
In effigy, through this favouring air
    Are hanging silks with dreams designed.

From those rich kingcups at the foot
Of soaring rock whence yew trees shoot
Up to the flashing swift pursuit
    Of cloud on cloud where stone cuts sky,
It might be peril's deadliest hold;
The wheeling rooks are much too bold,
To build there? but the trees unfold
    In tenderest green a sweet reply.

And see this stream that marches strong
With urgent and invincible song,
In myriad spearheads hurled along,
  Assailing, sallying, arrowing miles;
Immensely as his lordship roars,
He rides but into Oberon's wars,
Forget-me-not from both his shores
  Watches his wrath with blue-eyed smiles. . . .

From abbot's-kitchen caves aloft
(I thought none lived there) cobweb-soft
A mystery grows, the winds up-waft
  The smoke of an enchanter's fire;
But that enchanter proves no more
Than the boys' fancy who explore
His threshold, study and corridor,
  And gnome-like dart about his spire.

We here in grace have gladly passed
Beyond the world, behind us cast
Its tumult; for that Titan blast
  Which makes the cawing rooks unheard
Is this dream's own, and we float on
In dream-time, love and nature one,
Hand folding hand, as flower and sun,
  And wave and stone, and song and word.

EDMUND BLUNDEN, from 'Dovedale on a Spring Day'
Shells by a Stream, 1944

... AT THE time of which I write, when the light first sculptured for me the outlines of ridge after ridge, misty and tree-tufted, stretching away towards the heights, distant and unattainable, the landscape and its inhabitants possessed even more character than they do today. Then, as now, in the distance beyond the park, the great plumes of smoke would wave triumphantly over the pyramids of slag, down which, every now and then, crawled writhing serpents of fire, as the cinders were discharged from the trucks. After dark, this process at conjecturable intervals lit the whole night with a wild glory, so that, my father told me, standing on the lawn he could read his watch by the light of Staveley flares three miles away, and in the woods this sudden illumination gave an added poignance to the sylvan glades that it revealed, causing the rabbits to be frozen for an instant into immobility, their eyes reflecting the glare and the terror within them, showing a shape, which might be that of an otter from the lake below, scudding through the long wet grass, and making the great owl hiccup uneasily in the trees where formerly he had hooted with assurance. As the golden surge diminished, so did the uneasy stirring of the minute but multitudinous life beneath the tall bracken. ... All this is the same today – except that the immigrant small owl has made his way here and adds his clamour to the summer night; indeed, the flares are brighter. But in those times, during the hours of daylight, the very starkness of the little houses, and the blackness of them from the smoke – at which there had been no attempt at amelioration – added their own quality of outrageous contrast, even, as it were, of colour. In this *chiaroscuro* world, the gangs of miners returning from their work would tramp along the roads, wearing stuttering clogs, cord trousers and scarlet tunics, the cast-off tunics of a happy army, then still dressed in musical-comedy uniforms, which the colliers bought regularly; a costume which set off the blackness of their faces and their scarlet lips. . . .

In the hot summer the house, standing above the world on its wide table-land, threw its battlemented and spired shadow, uncompromising and stark for all its fantasy, as far as the tall beech trees at the hills' edge, while down below, in the north park, the golden mist still lay melting. On this side, the house makes no gesture to the graces, but is a stout-built, machicolated screen with but a few shallow breaks in the hundred yards of its façade. Here is no garden, only the grass and the old trees, of great girth; in spite of its austerity, it is rustic and pastoral, cows and horses come out of the Palladian stables into the park, and in their seasons buttercups and mushrooms grow among the green tufts of the turf. But on the south side, the atmosphere changes dramatically, is no longer pastoral but romantic. The house with its deep recesses, the fountains and pools and hedges set so fast among their surrounding woods that in the distance from the south the building appears to rise from a forest, the vistas to which lead every alley and every green court, are all part of the great romantic movement; and water provides the link which binds them together, water dripping from fountains and flashing from pools and culminating in the expanse of lake below, that swoons in a summer ecstasy of sun-born mist and still green leaves to the nostalgic rhythms of Mendelssohn, Weber, Chopin and Tchaikovsky.

SIR OSBERT SITWELL
Right Hand, Left Hand, Vol. I, 1945

A VILLAGE IN OXFORDSHIRE

THE whole scene, the elaborate late-gothic church – large as a cathedral and with a spire too lofty even for so important a building as that – round which the little village, built of golden stone, its every house thatched and having mullion windows, congregated with a curious perfection on the slopes each side of a small stream, appeared to be set . . . in a perpetual springtide that belonged, because of the light and the perspective, because of the way the golden walls and buildings, with their roofs of thatch, looked against the landscape, and in spite of the fact that the country possessed hills, to the Dutch seventeenth-century masters or to the Flemish painters of an earlier time. The light had a golden edge to it, defined, yet ragged and hazy as the petals of giant sunflowers. And they, indeed, would have seemed the flowers most appropriate to beauty of this order, but my brother and I always arrived there in the season of primrose, daffodil and tulip. Then, the garden running down to the stream developed a special pre-Raphaelite charm that only belongs to small gardens in England, and, beyond that, to those situated by the side of water; each blossom, though the flowers grew in drifts, seemed separately illumined, prospering in its own nimbus of life-giving spring sunshine. Every bird showed the arc of its flight, every feather, in blue or green or russet, startled you with the soft purity of its colour, every branch, every twig, every leaf now unfolding in lily and silver and pale rose, retained still its own entity, its individual value, had not yet entered into the full symphony of green. It was the instant of spring equivalent to that at a concert before the conductor takes his place, when every musician in an orchestra for a moment or two practises his own instrument.

SIR OSBERT SITWELL, *The Scarlet Tree*, 1946

THE BEECHEN COOMBES

WHEN a hot sun has dried the woods the wind beats a cloud of pollen like grey smoke from the yews on the beechen coombes which are characteristic of Hampshire. They are steep-sided bays, running and narrowing far into and up the sides of the chalk hills, and especially of those hills with which the high flinty plateau breaks down to the greensand and the plain. These steep sides are clothed with beeches, thousands of beeches interrupted by the black yews that resemble caverns among the paler trees, or, in the spring, by the green haze of a few larches and the white flames of the beam tree buds. Sometimes a stream rises at the head of the coombe, and before its crystal is a yard wide and ankle deep over the crumbling chalk it is full of trout; the sunny ripples are meshed like honeycomb. If there is not a stream there is a hop garden, or there is a grassy floor approached by neither road nor path and crossed only by huntsman and hounds. All the year round the coombes, dripping, green and still, are cauldrons for the making and unmaking of mists, mists that lie like solid level snow or float diaphanous and horizontal of airiest silk across the moon or the morning sun. The coombes breed whole families, long genea-logical trees, of echoes which the child delights to call up from their light sleep; so, too, do fox and owl at night, and the cow on a calm evening; and as to the horn and the cry of hounds, the hangers entangle and repeat them as if they would imprison them for ever, so that the phantom exceeds the true. . . . The missel thrush rolls out his clear song. The woodpecker laughs his loud shaking laughter as he bounds in his flight. Among the golden green mistletoe in the old shaggy apple tree at the entrance of the coombe the blackbird sings, composing phrases all the sweeter for being strangely like some in the songs that countrymen used to sing.

EDWARD THOMAS, *The South Country*, 1909

ON ISIS' BANKS

THEN let the village bells, as often wont,
Come swelling on the breeze, and to the sun,
Half-set, sing merrily their ev'ning song.
I ask not for the cause. It matters not
What swain is wedded, what gay lass is bound
To love for aye, to cherish and obey.
It is enough for me to hear the sound
Of the remote exhilarating peal.
Now dying all away, now faintly heard,
And now with loud and musical relapse
Its mellow changes pouring on the ear.
So have I stood at eve on Isis' banks,
To hear the merry Christ-Church bells ring round.
So have I sat too in thy honour'd shades,
Distinguish'd Magdalen, on Charwell's brink,
To hear thy silver Wolsey tones so sweet.
And so too have I paus'd and held my oar,
And suffered the slow stream to bear me home,
While Wykeham's peal along the meadow ran.

REV. JAMES HURDIS
The Village Curate, 1788

IN THE BACKS

Too many of the dead, some I knew well,
Have smelt this unforgotten river smell,
Liquid and old and dank;
And on the tree-dark, lacquered, slowly passing stream
Have seen the boats come softly as in dream
Past the green bank.
So Camus, reverend sire, came footing slow
Three hundred years ago,
And Milton paced the avenue of trees
In miracle of sun and shade as now,
The fresh-attempted glorious cadences
Behind his youthful brow.

Milton and Chaucer, Herbert, Herrick, Gray,
Rupert, and you forgotten others, say —
Are there slow rivers and bridges where you have gone away?
What has your spirit found?
What wider lot?
Some days in spring do you come back at will,
And tread with weightless feet the ancient ground?
O say, if not,
Why is this air so sacred and so still?

FRANCES CORNFORD, *Travelling Home*, 1948

IN THE FENS

WANDERING by the river's edge,
I love to rustle through the sedge,
And through the woods of reed to tear
Almost as high as bushes are.
Yet, turning quick with shudder chill,
As danger ever does from ill,
Fear's moment-ague quakes the blood,
While plop the snake coils in the flood
And, hissing with a forkèd tongue,
Across the river winds along.
In coat of orange, green, and blue
Now on a willow branch I view,
Grey waving to the sunny gleam,
Kingfishers watch the ripple stream
For little fish that nimble by
And in the gravel shallows lie.
Eddies run before the boats,
Gurgling where the fisher floats,
Who takes advantage of the gale
And hoists his handkerchief for sail
On osier twigs that form a mast –
And quick his nutshell hurries past,
While idly lies, nor wanted more,
The sprit that pushed him on before.
There's not a hill in all the view,
Save that a forkèd cloud or two
Upon the verge of distance lies
And into mountains cheats the eyes. . . .

JOHN CLARE, *Poems,* 1920 (written *c.* 1833)

IN SAVERNAKE FOREST

How soothing sound the gentle airs that move
Th' innumerable leaves, high overhead,
When autumn first, from the long avenue,
That lifts its arching height of ancient shade,
Steals here and there a leaf!
       Within the gloom,
In partial sunshine white, some trunks appear,
Studding the glens of fern; in solemn shade
Some mingle their dark branches, but yet all, –
All make a sad sweet music, as they move,
Not undelightful to a stranger's heart.
They seem to say, in accents audible,
Farewell to summer, and farewell the strains
Of many a lithe and feathered chorister,
That through the depth of these incumbent woods
Made the long summer gladsome.
        I have heard
To the deep-mingling sounds of organs clear,
(When the slow choral anthem rose beneath),
The glimmering Minster, through its pillared aisles,
Echo; – but not more sweet the vaulted roof
Rang to those linked harmonies, than here
The high wood answers to the lightest breath
Of nature . . .

REV. WILLIAM LISLE BOWLES
Poems, Written Chiefly at Bremhill, in Wiltshire, 1809

THE VILLAGE AT REST

How still the morning of the hallow'd day!
Mute is the voice of rural labour, hush'd
The ploughboy's whistle, and the milkmaid's song.
The scythe lies glittering in the dewy wreath
Of tedded grass, mingled with fading flowers
That yester-morn bloom'd waving in the breeze:
The faintest sounds attract the ear – the hum
Of early bee, the trickling of the dew,
The distant bleating, midway up the hill,
Calmness seems throned on yon unmoving cloud.
To him who wanders o'er the upland leas,
The blackbird's note comes mellower from the dale;
And sweeter from the sky the gladsome lark
Warbles his heaven-tuned song; the lulling brook
Murmurs more gently down the deep-worn glen;
While from yon lowly roof, whose curling smoke
O'ermounts the mist, is heard, at intervals,
The voice of psalms, the simple song of praise.

　　With dove-like wings, Peace o'er yon village broods;
The dizzying mill-wheel rests; the anvil's din
Hath ceased; all, all around is quietness.
Less fearful on this day, the limping hare
Stops, and looks back, and stops, and looks on man,
Her deadliest foe.　The toil-worn horse, set free,
Unheedful of the pasture, roams at large;
And, as his stiff unwieldly bulk he rolls,
His iron-arm'd hoofs gleam in the morning-ray . . .

REV. JAMES GRAHAME, *The Sabbath*, 1804

CRANCE TO A VILLAGE: WATERCOLOUR DRAWING BY THOMAS ROWLANDSON

CORRA LYNN, ON THE CLYDE: WATERCOLOUR DRAWING BY JOHN WHITE ABBOTT, 1791

BY THE BANKS OF CLYDE

I SAW the liquid snowy mountains rolled
Prone down the awful steep; I heard the din
That shook the hill, from caves that boiled within. . . .
Here let me walk abroad when tempests fly,
And careless hear them rage along the sky;
Where forest trees with daring grandeur rise,
Disdain the earth, and bold invade the skies.
How wide his arms the stately oak extends!
The plane's thick head 'mid burning day suspends
Impenetrable shade; bees humming pour
O'er the broad balmy leaves and suck the flower.
Green shoots the fir his spiry point on high;
And fluttering leaves on trembling aspens sigh;
With haughtier air, see the strong oak ascend,
Too proud before an angry heaven to bend:
His leaves unshaken, winter's rage defy;
He shades a field, and heaves a wood on high;
Glories in stubborn strength, when tempests roar,
And scorns to yield, save to the thunder's power.

JOHN WILSON, *Clyde*, 1764

DAWN OVER BERKSHIRE

ABOVE yon sombre swell of land
   Thou see'st the dawn's grave orange hue,
With one pale streak like yellow sand,
   And over that a vein of blue.

The air is cold above the woods;
   All silent is the earth and sky,
Except with his own lonely moods
   The blackbird holds a colloquy.

Over the broad hill creeps a beam,
   Like hope that gilds a good man's brow;
And now ascends the nostril-steam
   Of stalwart horses come to plough . . .

RICHARD HENRY HORNE
from 'The Plough'
Cosmo de Medici, 1875

SUNSET ON CARRONBEN

O, THE sweet melancholy of the time
When gently, ere the heart appeals, the year
Shines in the fatal beauty of decay!
When the sun sinks enlarged on Carronben,
Nakedly visible, without a cloud,
And faintly from the faint eternal blue
(That dim, sweet harebell-colour) comes the star
Which evening wears; – when Luggie flows in mist,
And in the cottage windows, one by one,
With sudden twinkle household lamps are lit,
What noiseless falling of the faded leaf!

DAVID GRAY
The Luggie and other Poems, 1862

93

DOWN IN DEVON

THIS onward-deepening gloom – this hanging path
Over the Linn that soundeth mightily,
Foaming and tumbling on, as if in wrath
That aught should bar its passage to the sea,
These sundered walls of rock, tier upon tier
Built darkly up into the very sky,
Hung with thick woods, the native haunt of deer
And sheep that browse the dizzy slopes on high –
All half-unreal to my fancy seem, –
For opposite my crib, long years ago,
Were pictured just such rocks, just such a stream,
With just this height above, and depth below;
Even this jutting crag I seem to know –
As when some sight calls back a half-forgotten dream.

REV. HENRY ALFORD
'Linn Cleeve, Linton, Devon', *Poetical Works*, 1845

HEART OF MIDLOTHIAN

Most lovely was the verdure of the hills –
A rich, luxuriant green, o'er which the sky
Of blue, translucent, clear without a cloud,
Outspread its arching amplitude serene.
With many a gush of music, from each brake
Sang forth the choral linnets; and the lark,
Ascending from the clover field, by fits
Soared as it sang, and dwindled from the sight.
The cushat stood amidst the topmost boughs
Of the tall tree, his white-ringed neck aslant,
Down thro' the leaves to see his brooding mate.
'Mid the tall meadow-grass the ox reclined,
Or bent his knee, or from beneath the shade
Of the broad beech, with ruminant mouth, gazed forth.
Rustling with wealth, a tissue of fair fields
Outstretched to left and right in luxury;
And the fir forests on the upland slopes
Contrasted darkly with the golden grain.

DAVID MACBETH MOIR, from 'The Angler'
Poetical Works, 1852

THE BELLS OF FIFE

THE fair Earth laughs through all her boundless range,
   Heaving her green hills high to greet the beam;
City and village, steeple, cot and grange,
   Gilt as with nature's purest leaf-gold seem;
The heaths and upland muirs, and fallows, change
   Their barren brown into a ruddy gleam,
And, on ten thousand dew-bent leaves and sprays,
Twinkle ten thousand suns and fling their petty rays.

Up from their nests and fields of tender corn
   Full merrily the little sky-larks spring,
And on their dew-bedabbled pinions born,
   Mount to the heav'n's blue key-stone flickering;
They turn their plume-soft bosoms to the morn,
   And hail the genial light and cheerly sing;
Echo the gladsome hills and valleys round,
And half the bells of Fife ring loud and swell the sound. . . .

And, from our steeple's pinnacle outspread,
   The town's long colours flare and flap on high,
Whose anchor, blazoned fair in green and red,
   Curls, pliant to each breeze that whistles by;
Whilst on the boltsprit stern and topmast-head
   Of brig and and sloop that in the harbour lie,
Streams the red gaudery of flags in air
All to salute and grace the morn of Anster Fair.

WILLIAM TENNANT, *Anster Fair*, 1812

CHIME IN THE MENDIPS

How grand beneath the feet that company
   Of steep grey roofs and clustering pinnacles
Of the massy fane, brooding in majesty
   Above the town that spreads among the dells!
Hark! the deep clock unrolls its voice of power;
   And sweetly-mellowed sound of chiming bells
Calling to prayer from out the central tower
   Over the thickly-timbered hollow dwells.
Meet worship-place for such a glorious stretch
   Of sunny prospect – for these mighty hills,
And that dark solemn Tor, and all that reach
   Of bright-green meadows, laced with silver rills,
Bounded by ranges of pale blue, that rise
To where white strips of sea are traced upon the skies.

REV. HENRY ALFORD
'The Mendip Hills over Wells'
Poetical Works, 1845

ON THE MOUNTAIN

... THE UPWARD climbs through the dark plantations, beside the rock-walled stream; the tramp over the upland pastures, one gay flower-bed of blue and purple butter-wort; the steady breathless climb up the crags, which looked but one mile from you when you started, so clear against the sky stood out every knoll and slab; the first stars of the white saxifrage, golden-eyed, blood-bedropt, as if a fairy had pricked her finger in the cup, which shine upon some green cushion of wet moss, in a dripping crack of the cliff; the first gray tufts of the Alpine club-moss, the first shrub of crowberry, or sea-green rose-root, with its strange fleshy stems and leaves, which mark the two-thousand-feet-line, and the beginning of the Alpine world; the scramble over the arid waves of the porphyry sea aloft, as you beat round and round like a weary pointer dog in search of the hidden lake; the last despairing crawl to the summit of the Syenite pyramid on Moel Meirch; the hasty gaze around, far away into the green vale of Ffestiniog, and over wooded flats, and long silver river-reaches, and yellow sands, and blue sea flecked with flying clouds, and isles and capes, and wildernesses of mountain peaks, east, west, south and north; one glance at the purple gulf out of which Snowdon rises, thence only seen in full majesty from base to peak; and then the joyful run, springing over bank and boulder, to the sad tarn beneath your feet; the loosening of the limbs as you toss yourself, bathed in perspiration, on the turf; the almost awed pause as you recollect that you are alone on the mountain-tops, by the side of the desolate pool, out of all hope of speech or help of man; and, if you break your leg among those rocks, may lie there till the ravens pick your bones ...

REV. CHARLES KINGSLEY, 'Chalk-stream Studies'
in *Fraser's Magazine*, September 1858

OWDON FROM LLYN NANTLLE: PAINTING BY RICHARD WILSON, R.A., *c.* 1766

A WOOSEMAN, OR MAN OF THE WOODS: WOOD-CARVING IN THE BULL INN, LONG MELFORD

FIGURES
IN A LANDSCAPE

I SEE the wagons move along the rows
   Of ripe and summer-breathing clover-flower,
I see the lissom husbandman who knows
   Deep in his heart the beauty of his power,
As, lithely pitched, the full-heaped fork bids on
   The harvest home. I hear the rickyard fill
With gossip as in generations gone,
   While wagon follows wagon from the hill.
I think how, when our seasons all are sealed,
Shall come the unchanging harvest from the field.

I see the barns and comely manors planned
   By men who somehow moved in comely thought,
Who, with a simple shippon to their hand,
   As men upon some godlike business wrought;
I see the little cottages that keep
   Their beauty still where since Plantagenet
Have come the shepherds happily to sleep,
   Finding the loaves and cups of cider set;
I see the twisted shepherds, brown and old,
Driving at dusk their glimmering sheep to fold.

JOHN DRINKWATER, *Tides*, 1917

MANY HARMONIES

THE country habit has me by the heart.
I never hear the sheep-bells in the fold,
Nor see the ungainly heron rise and flap
Over the marsh, nor hear the asprous corn
Clash, as the reapers set the sheaves in shocks
(That like a tented army dream away
The night beneath the moon in silvered fields),
Nor watch the stubborn team of horse and man
Graven upon the skyline, nor regain
The sign-posts on the roads towards my home
Bearing familiar names – without a strong
Leaping of recognition; only here
Lies peace after uneasy truancy;
Here meet and marry many harmonies,
– All harmonies being ultimately one, -
Small mirroring majestic; for as earth
Rolls on her journey, so her little fields
Ripen or sleep, and the necessities
Of seasons match the planetary law.
So truly stride between the earth and heaven
Sowers of grain: so truly in the spring
Earth's orbit swings both blood and sap to rhythm,
And infinite and humble are at one;
So the brown hedger, through the evening lanes
Homeward returning, sees above the ricks,
Sickle in hand, the sickle in the sky. . . .

V. SACKVILLE-WEST, *The Land*, 1926

MERRY ENGLAND

THE beams of the morning sun shining on the lonely glades, or through the idle branches of the tangled forest, the leisure, the freedom, 'the pleasure of going and coming without knowing where,' the troops of wild deer, the sports of the chase, and other rustic gambols, were sufficient to justify the well-known appellation of 'Merry Sherwood', and in like manner, we may apply the phrase to Merry England. The smile is not the less sincere because it does not always play upon the cheek; and the jest is not the less welcome, nor the laugh less hearty, because they happen to be a relief from care or leaden-eyed melancholy. The instances are the more precious as they are rare; and we look forward to them with the greater goodwill, or back upon them with the greater gratitude, as we drain the last drop in the cup with particular relish. . . .

'Continents,' says Hobbes, 'have most of what they contain' – and in this view it may be contended that the English are the merriest people in the world, since they only show it on high-days and holidays. They are then like a school-boy let loose from school, or like a dog that has slipped his collar. They are not gay like the French, who are one eternal smile of self-complacency, tortured into affectation, or spun into languid indifference, nor are they voluptuous and immersed in sensual indolence, like the Italians; but they have that sort of intermittent, fitful, irregular gaiety, which is neither worn out by habit, nor deadened by passion, but is sought with avidity as it takes the mind by surprise, is startled by a sense of oddity and incongruity, indulges its wayward humours or lively impulses with perfect freedom and lightness of heart, and seizes occasion by the forelock, that it may return to serious business with more cheerfulness, and have something to beguile the hours of thought or sadness.

WILLIAM HAZLITT, *Sketches and Essays*, 1839

103

FAIRGROUND

... CRESCENDO symphony of penny joys
With counterpoint on counterpoint of noise –
The thwack of balls against the ninepin sheet,
The crunch of cinders under shuffled feet,
The power-impelling engine's rhythmic choke,
The bell that answers swaggered mallet's stroke,
The crang of shots that rake the rifle-range,
And chinking undertone of copper change.
The crowd is thickest round the switch-back's race,
With castanetting wheels, the blur of face,
The rushing round the bends to overtop
The heart-arresting, stomach-stealing drop:
There, organ-throned on high, the chip-faced gods
Still give their little, haughty, clockwork nods –
The hurdy-gurdy, steam-pulsed music stammers
With plinking of their rounded metal hammers.
The sparky hissing of the naphtha flares
Still haunts the thoughts of all my Autumn Fairs,
'The Greatest, Finest Fun-Fair In The Land'.
My coppers tightly clenched in sweaty hand,
There's colour here, and only colour counts,
Those red-lipped stallions are my chosen mounts:
To saddle then, with fancied Cossack spring,
And, knees to flanks and hands to reins I cling,
While, breathless, up and down and round and round
My pure-white steed careers in full-stretch bound;
I look around in dizzy horseman's pride
And scorn those earth-bound crowds who do not ride . . .

JOHN ARLOTT, *Of Period and Place*, 1944

AGRICULTURAL SHOW: WATERCOLOUR DRAWING BY EDWARD BAWDEN, R.A., 1947

SHOW RING

In a corner of the show, farm machinery reared itself like primitive artillery against a bastion of trees. We went to inspect this section, as it was not yet time for the horses to be paraded round the ring. Small oil-engines coughed and spluttered here, while the flywheels of large traction-engines revolved slowly with the faintest hissing from the engine, and their drivers clambered about them with oily rags. There were threshing-drums, binders, elevators, wagons, tumbrils, painted boldly red and blue. Mr. Colville noted improvements here and there in details, was nearly persuaded into buying a tractor, but moved away without finally committing himself, even though he had knocked something off the list price, saying, 'I'll think it over and let you know'.

As we returned towards the ring we paused at the butter-making competition. Here, beneath an awning roof, spick and span maidens were turning the handles of churns or lifting off the lids and looking inside. A cool smell floated out to us from there. Though they worked hard, they contrived somehow to appear cool, and, despite the exertion and the fashion of the day, they were rounded in face and figure. Their cheeks were rosy and their bare arms comely and vigorous.

Now we return to the ring. The music languishes and surges lazily. The flags set round the ring on crimson-bound staffs swoon and rally, unfolding continually like scrolls. The boughs of trees lift and fall, sending cataracts of shadows across the roofs of the pavilions. The heavy horses are being paraded. The Suffolks come first, plump and glossy. Sometimes they break into a tense, slow trot, as though to ease an overflow of strength. Then they hardly seem to touch the ground, like fabled creatures working an aerial treadmill for the gods.

After them come the Shire horses, ponderous living machinery, magnificent and ungainly. The hair spreading about their hoofs gives their legs a tree-trunk sturdiness. Their manes and tails are plaited and beribboned, and they wear halters of red or yellow leather studded with brass that flashes starrily when they toss their heads. A man leads each horse, twitching the rein occasionally. There are old men walking with rolling rustic unconcern and younger ones with traces of army bearing, whose unnatural sternness of expression marks the importance of the day for them.

Now a prize-winner passes, a rosette upon his temple, and a rumble of applause goes round the ring.

Now come mares with foals whinnying and prancing at their sides, now yearlings in the gawkiness of youth, but giving promise of future greatness.

Still they come, a lumbering Armada of horses, approaching from beyond the dark masses of the people opposite, their heads nodding against a white background of tents as they walk. The band plays them all in, seems to play also those gay white clouds across the sky.

At length the whole ring is full. The horses are halted in a vast regiment facing the grand stand, some pawing the ground, others with feet well spread, immovable as rocks. With deeply arched necks and shining flanks and ebony hoofs, they are like some old peace-offering between kings. There is a munificence that is Arabian here in the heat and fierce light. . . .

ADRIAN BELL, *Corduroy*, 1930

THE BEAUTY OF TOOLS

THE beauty of tools is not accidental, but inherent and essential. The contours of a ship's sail bellying in the wind are not more inevitable, nor more graceful, than the curves of an adze-head or of a plough-share. Cast in iron or steel, the gracefulness of a plough-share is more indestructible than the metal, yet pliant (within the limits of its type) as a line of English blank verse. It changes for different soils: it is widened out or narrowed; it is deep-grooved or shallow; not because of caprice at the foundry or to satisfy an artistic fad, but to meet the technical demands of the expert ploughman. The most familiar example of beauty indicating subtle technique is supplied by the admired shape of boats, which, however, is so variable (the statement is made on the authority of an old coast-guardsman) that the boat best adapted for one stretch of shore may be dangerous, if not entirely useless, at another stretch ten miles away. And as technique determines the design of a boat, or of a waggon, or of a plough-share, so it controls absolutely the fashioning of tools. . . .

Quarryman's peck, coachman's whip, cricket-bat, fishing-rod, trowel, all have their intimate relation to the skill of those who use them; and like animals and plants adapting themselves each to its own place in the universal order, they attain to beauty by force of being fit. That law of adaptation which shapes the wings of a swallow and prescribes the poise and elegance of the branches of trees, is the same that demands symmetry in the corn-rick and convexity in the beer-barrel; the same that, exerting itself with matchless precision through the trained senses of haymakers and woodmen, gives the final curve to the handles of their scythes and the shafts of their axes. Hence the beauty of a tool is an unfailing sign that in the proper handling of it technique is present.

GEORGE BOURNE, *Lucy Bettesworth*, 1913

PLOUGHING

A CREAKING and metallic rattle, as of chains, comes across the arable field – a steady gaze reveals the dim outline of a team of horses slowly dragging the plough, their shapes indistinctly seen against the hedge. A bent figure follows, and by-and-by another distinct creak and rattle, and yet a third in another direction, show that there are more teams at work, plodding to and fro. Watching their shadowy forms, suddenly the eye catches a change in the light somewhere. Over the meadow yonder the mist is illuminated; it is not sunshine, but a white light, only visible by contrast with the darker mist around. It lasts a few moments, and then moves, and appears a second time by the copse. Though hidden here, the disk of the sun must be partly visible there, and as the white light does not remain long in one place, it is evident that there is motion now in the vast mass of vapour. Looking upwards there is the faintest suspicion of the palest blue, dull and dimmed by mist, so faint that its position cannot be fixed, and the next instant it is gone again.

But the teams at plough are growing momentarily distinct – a breath of air touches the cheek, then a leaf breaks away from the bough and starts forth as if bent on a journey, but loses the impetus and sinks to the ground. Soon afterwards the beams of the sun light up a distant oak that glows in the hedge – a rich deep buff – and it stands out, clear, distinct, and beautiful, the chosen and selected one, the first to receive the ray. Rapidly the mist vanishes – disappearing rather than floating away; a circle of blue sky opens overhead, and, finally, travelling slowly, comes the sunshine over the furrows.

RICHARD JEFFERIES, *Hodge and his Masters*, 1880

MOWING

BETWEEN two golden tufts of summer grass
I see the world through hot air as through glass,
And by my face sweet lights and colours pass.

Before me, dark against the fading sky,
I watch three mowers mowing, as I lie:
With brawny arms they sweep in harmony.

Brown English faces by the sun burnt red,
Rich glowing colour on bare throat and head,
My heart would leap to watch them, were I dead!

And in my strong young living as I lie,
I seem to move with them in harmony –
A fourth is mowing, and that fourth am I.

The music of the scythes that glide and leap,
The young men whistling as their great arms sweep,
And all the perfume and sweet sense of sleep.

The weary butterflies that droop their wings,
The dreamy nightingale that hardly sings,
And all the lassitude of happy things,

Is mingling with the warm and pulsing blood,
That gushes through my veins a languid flood,
And feeds my spirit as the sap a bud. . . .

SIR EDMUND GOSSE, *On Viol and Flute,* 1873

III

LOVE IN THE GREEN GLEN

LOVE, meet me in the green glen,
  Beside the tall elm-tree,
Where the sweetbrier smells so sweet agen;
  There come with me,
    Meet me in the green glen.

Meet me at the sunset
  Down in the green glen,
Where we've often met
  By hawthorn-tree and foxes' den,
    Meet me in the green glen.

Meet me in the green glen,
  By sweetbrier bushes there;
Meet me by your own sen,
  Where the wild thyme blossoms fair.
    Meet me in the green glen.

Meet me by the sweetbrier,
  By the mole-hill swelling there;
Where the west glows like a fire
  God's crimson bed is there.
    Meet me in the green glen.

JOHN CLARE, *Poems*, 1920
(written *c.* 1850)

LOVE IN A VALLEY

TAKE me, Lieutenant, to that Surrey homestead!
   Red comes the winter and your rakish car,
Red among the hawthorns, redder than the hawberries
   Or trails of old man's nuisance, and noisier far.
Far, far below me roll the Coulsdon woodlands,
   White down the valley curves the living rail,
Tall, tall, above me, olive spike the pinewoods,
   Olive against blue-black, moving in the gale.

Deep down the drive go the cushioned rhododendrons,
   Deep down, sand deep, drives the heather root,
Deep the spliced timber barked around the summer-house,
   Light lies the tennis-court, plantain underfoot.
What a winter welcome to what a Surrey homestead!
   Oh! the metal lantern and white enamelled door!
Oh! the spread of orange from the gas-fire on the carpet!
   Oh! the tiny patter, sandalled footsteps on the floor!

Fling wide the curtains! – there's a Surrey sunset!
   Low down the line sings the Addiscombe train,
Leaded are the windows lozenging the crimson,
   Drained dark the pines on resin-scented rain.
Portable Lieutenant! they carry you to China
   And me to lonely shopping in a brilliant arcade;
Firm hand, fond hand, switch the giddy engine!
   So for us a last time is bright light made.

JOHN BETJEMAN, *Continual Dew*, 1937

WHEELS

JUST as a biologist may see, in any limpet, signs of the rocky shore, the smashing breakers, so the provincial wheelwright could hardly help reading, from the waggon-lines, tales of haymaking and upland fields, of hilly roads and lonely woods and noble horses, and so on. The age-long effort of Englishmen to fit themselves close and ever closer into England was betokened in my old farm-waggon; and this the little puffing steam-tractor seemed to flout.

But where begin to describe so efficient an organism, in which all the parts interacted until it is hard to say which was modified first, to meet which other? Was it to suit the horses or the ruts, the loading or the turning, that the front wheels had to have a diameter of about four feet? Or was there something in the average height of a carter, or in the skill of wheel-makers, that fixed these dimensions? One only knew that, by a wonderful compromise, all these points had been provided for in the country tradition of fore-wheels for a waggon. . . . In these and a hundred details every well-built farm-waggon (of whatever variety) was like an organism, reflecting in every curve and dimension some special need of its own country-side. . . . In farm-yard, in tap-room, at market, the details were discussed over and over again; they were gathered together for remembrance in village workshop; carters, smiths, farmers, wheel-makers, in thousands handed on each his own little bit of understanding, passing it to his son or to the wheelwright of the day, linking up the centuries. But for the most part the details were but dimly understood; the whole body of knowledge was a mystery, a piece of folk knowledge, residing in the folk collectively, but never wholly in any individual.

GEORGE STURT, *The Wheelwright's Shop*, 1923

ARM WAGGON: PAINTING BY TRISTRAM HILLIER, 1943

MR AND MRS ROBERT ANDREWS: PAINTING BY THOMAS GAINSBOROUGH, R.A., *c.* 1749

THRESHING: PAINTING BY JOHN NASH, R.A., 1915

STEAM

OUR children will know only the tractor and the combine harvester, but, just as an older generation could recall with nostalgia the thwack of the flail on the threshing floor, so we shall remember always that plume of steam over the stackyard on misty autumn mornings and the drone of the threshing drum rising and falling as the sheaves were fed in.

L. T. C. ROLT, in *The Saturday Book*, 1955

CARTED away are all the leaning stooks,
And from the stackyard comes the thresher's purr.
England's a humming hive till threshing's done,
And chaff-motes blowing from the emptied sacks
Mellow the barn in beams of dusty sun.
Threshing's a game which sets the farm astir
On fine October mornings when the mist
Melts to reveal between the steaming stacks
The thresher lumbering slowly up the lane.
The gang swarms out in jolly morning vein;
Unricker, leather strap about his wrist,
Sackman, and stacker, and the loutish hands,
And dairymaid, agreeable to be kissed,
And farmer's wife, come out to see the fun
After a week of baking loaf and pie,
Admires the young men with a roguish eye;
And barn-door hens that pick among the grain
And terrier nosing round for rats, and bands
Of children, rather shy.

V. SACKVILLE-WEST, *The Land*, 1926

119

CHURCH FÊTE

Roll up, roll up to our Church Fête.
Sixpence will get you through the gate,
Or if you boggle at expense,
Sneak through our fence
And crawl
Into our rummage stall.
We can supply
An old Etonian tie
Or backless gown
For threepence down,
With Mrs. Hepplewhite's stuffed duck
Flung in for luck.
Roll up, it's time you went
Into the tent
And saw
The one original great niece-in-law
Of Gipsy Lee,
Who for a modest fee
(In tones that to the life
Echo our postman's wife)
Repeats embarrassingly fast
Your past,
But is particularly dumb
About what is to come.
Roll up and win
A gilded safety-pin
For loosing a balloon
To Finchley or Rangoon,

Provided that the natives aren't too slack
To send it back.
Roll up your sleeve
And heave
A frenzied ball
Into the glass and china stall
In an attempt to uppercut
A coco-nut.
Roll up, but make no rash mistake;
It's Mrs. Brown's fruit-cake,
Not Mrs. Brown whose weight
Is the keen subject of debate.
Roll up, or walk if you prefer;
Do not demur
About it being wet;
Try to forget
As best you can
That every honest Englishman
Hates
Fêtes.

DANIEL PETTIWARD, *Truly Rural*, 1939

DOWN TO THE DERBY

TWIGGERY, swiggery, shinery, finery, laughery,
  chaffery, pokery, jokery –
Down to the Derby as all of us go,
These are the sights that we each of us know;
Yet off to the Downs as we often have been,
Still every year is some novelty seen.

Epsom at last, nearing it fast,
  Smackery, crackery, whip, whip;
There's the Grand Stand, now close at hand,
  Think it a nice little trip, trip.
Get a good view, this one will do,
  Squeezing it, seizing it, rush, rush:
Downs looking smooth, CARELESS's Booth,
  Go in and get a good brush, brush.
Every one here, seems to appear,
  'How d'ye do?' 'How are you?' nod, nod.
Some friends about, can't find 'em out,
  Look for them, hook for them, odd, odd.

Smackery, snackery, scenery, greenery, Leger bit,
  hedge a bit, look about, shook about –
Down to the Derby as all of us go,
There are the sights that we each of us know;
Yet off to the Downs as we often have been,
Still every year is some novelty seen.

Now take your place, this is the race,
  Universe, tune averse, fame, fame;
Cards to be sold, everything told,
  Colours of riders and name, name.
Buzz! off they go, galloping so,
  Bothery, dothery, eye, eye;
Look as they pass, out with the glass,
  Can't find the focus to spy, spy,
Yonder they run, some horse has won,
  Up with the number and see, see;
Whichever is in, hundreds may win,
  But thousands will diddled like me be.

Cantering, bantering, cheering 'em, nearing 'em,
  spy away, flyaway, dothery, bothery –
Down to the Derby as all of us go,
These are the sights that we each of us know;
Yet off to the Downs as we often have been,
Still every year is some novelty seen . . .

SIR WILLIAM SCHWENK GILBERT
Lost Bab Ballads, 1932
(written *c.* 1875)

SHAPES AND VOICES

LEANING on the sun-blistered white paint of the window-ledge, I must enjoy my final stare at the garden; listen to the stable clock striking twelve; hear the clink of a bucket as the stable-boy finishes washing the carriage-wheels, and then one of the horses neighing and snorting while the coachman goes to the corn bin with his sieve. From somewhere beyond a yew hedge comes a murmur of voices, talking contentedly as people do while sitting out of doors on a fine summer day – talking, I like to think, about the new standard roses which have done so well this year; with an afterword that perhaps it *would* be as well to have iced-coffee besides claret-cup for the small tennis party this afternoon. . . .

SIEGFRIED SASSOON, *The Weald of Youth*, 1942

THE air is full of subdued frost, yet fog lies like cotton-wool upon the surface of the earth. In the afternoon I went out walking. Cold and dense indeed was the mist, but sounds travelled far through it, for I could hear the call of a distant partridge with wonderful distinctness, and although it must have been a mile or more away, the bark of a dog seemed so loud as to be almost startling. A man was in the field on my right, and quite invisible; yet my ear could catch every clink of the fork which he was using to spread manure. In the field to the left one of my ploughmen and his horses suddenly loomed up beyond the fence, then they turned, and before they had gone five yards grew dim and vanished in the soft, white cloud. A flock of sparrows crossed the road with a hush of wings, passing just above my head, for they did not see me. In an instant they were come and gone, through for a long while I could still distinguish the beating of their wings upon the heavy air.

SIR H. RIDER HAGGARD, *A Gardener's Year*, 1905

HOLY HOUR

Now the holy hour is nigh,
   Seek we out the holy ground;
Overhead the breezy sky,
   Rustling woodlands all around;
Fragrant steams from oak-leaves sere,
   Peat and moss and whortles green,
Dews that yet are glistening clear
   Through their brown or briary screen.

Hie we through the autumnal wood,
   Pausing where the echoes dwell,
Boys, or men of boyish mood,
   Trying how afar they swell.
Haply down some opening glade
   Now the old grey tower we see,
Underneath whose solemn shade
   Jesus risen hath sworn to be.

He hath sworn, for there will meet
   Two or three in His great name,
Waiting till their incense sweet,
   Feel His heaven-descended flame.
Day by day that old grey tower
   Tells its tale, and week by week
In their tranquil hoary bower
   To the unlearned its shadows speak.

REV. JOHN KEBLE
Lyra Innocentium, 1846

DETAIL

WHEN the Present has latched its postern behind my tremulous stay,
   And the May month flaps its glad green leaves like wings,
Delicate-filmed as new-spun silk, will the neighbours say,
   'He was a man who used to notice such things'?

If it be in the dusk when, like an eyelid's soundless blink,
   The dewfall-hawk comes crossing the shades to alight
Upon the wind-warped upland thorn, a gazer may think,
   'To him this must have been a familiar sight'.

If I pass during some nocturnal blackness, mothy and warm,
   When the hedgehog travels furtively over the lawn,
One may say, 'He strove that such innocent creatures should come
   to no harm,
   But he could do little for them; and now he is gone'.

If, when hearing that I have been stilled at last, they stand at the door,
   Watching the full-starred heavens that winter sees,
Will this thought rise on those who will meet my face no more,
   'He was one who had an eye for such mysteries'?

And will any say when my bell of quittance is heard in the gloom,
   And a crossing breeze cuts a pause in its outrollings,
Till they rise again, as they were a new bell's boom,
   'He hears it not now, but used to notice such things'?

THOMAS HARDY, 'Afterwards'
Collected Poems, 1919

NBRIDGE POND: PAINTING BY PAUL NASH, 1928

LANDSCAPE: WATERCOLOUR DRAWING BY SIR ANTHONY VAN DYCK, *c.* 1635

THE NATIVE MUSE

I LOVE the verse that, mild and bland,
   Breathes of green fields and open sky,
I love the muse that in her hand
   Bears flowers of native poesy;
Who walks nor skips the pasture brook
   In scorn, but by the drinking horse
Leans o'er its little brig to look
   How far the sallows lean across,

And feels a rapture in her breast
   Upon their root-fringed grains to mark
A hermit moorhen's sedgy nest
   Just like a naiad's summer bark.
She counts the eggs she cannot reach,
   Admires the spot and loves it well,
And yearns, so nature's lessons teach,
   Amid such neighbourhoods to dwell.

I love the muse who sits her down
   Upon the molehill's little lap,
Who feels no fear to stain her gown
   And pauses by the hedgerow gap;
Not with that affectation. praise
   Of song, to sing and never see
A field flower grow in all her days
   Or e'en a forest's aged tree.

JOHN CLARE, from 'The Flitting'
Poems, 1908 (written *c.* 1832)

THE SEEING EYE

RAIN falls, and in upright grey sheaves passes slowly before the fresh beech leaves like ghosts in shadowy procession; and once again the white clouds roll over the tops of the trees, and the green is virginal, and out of the drip and glimmer of the miles of blissful country rises the blackbird's song and the cuckoo's shout. The rain seems not only to have brightened what is to be seen but the eye that sees and the mind that knows, and suddenly we are aware of all the joy in the grandeur and mastery of an oak's balance, in those immobile clouds revealed on the farthest horizon shaped like the mountains which a child imagines, in the white candles of the beam tree, in the black-eyed bird sitting in her nest in the hawthorn with uplifted beak, and in the myriad luxuriant variety of shape and texture and bright colour in the divided leaves of wood sanicle and moschatel and parsley and cranesbill, in the pure outline of twayblade and violet and garlic. Newly dressed in the crystal of the rain the landscape recalls the earlier spring; the flowers of white wood-sorrel, the pink and white anemone and cuckoo flower, the thick-clustered, long-stalked primroses and darker cowslips with their scentless sweetness pure as an infant's breath; the solitary wild cherry trees flowering among still leafless beech; the blackbirds of twilight and the flower-faced owls; the pewits wheeling after dusk; the jonquil and daffodil and arabis and leopard's bane of cottage gardens; the white clouds plunged in blue floating over the brown woods of the hills; the delicate thrushes with speckled breasts paler than their backs, motion-less on dewy turf; and all the joys of life that come through the nostrils from the dark, not understood world which is unbolted for us by the delicate and savage fragrances of leaf and flower and grass and clod, of the plumage of birds and fur of animals . . .

EDWARD THOMAS, *The South Country*, 1909

A GENTLER heaven steals over the hour,
  And at its pace I go
  And scan green things that grow
Beneath old hedge and ivy-bower.
Most gracious falls the silent hour.

Through the shut sky an eye of blue
  Twinkles upon the soul,
  Even as these weeds unroll
Their leaves aspiring, choice and new;
Their greenness blesses, and that blue.

The round leaf, shield leaf, patterned spray
  All shine like love's first tears,
  And though no primrose peers,
Nor aconites, nor windflowers play,
I have their message through leaf and spray.

This may not be the hour I supposed
  When from the house I came
  Informed of a world aflame;
That will have been an era closed,
Though endless as I then supposed.

O green leaves born in winter's heart,
  White ghosts of flowers to be,
  Come here so quietly,
And blossoming heaven's blue counterpart,
– I have lost my way, and found my heart.

EDMUND BLUNDEN, 'God's Time'
Shells by a Stream, 1944

STONE

STERILE these stones
By time in ruin laid.
Yet many a creeping thing
Its haven has made
In these least crannies, where falls
Dark's dew, and noonday shade.

The claw of the tender bird
Finds lodgement here;
Dye-winged butterflies poise;
Emmet and beetle steer
Their busy course; the bee
Drones, laden, near.

Their myriad-mirrored eyes
Great day reflect.
By their exquisite farings
Is this granite specked;
Is trodden to infinite dust;
By gnawing lichens decked.

Toward what eventual dream
Sleeps its cold on,
When into ultimate dark
These lives shall be gone,
And even of man not a shadow remain
Of all he has done?

WALTER DE LA MARE, 'The Corner Stone'
The Veil and Other Poems, 1921

FOUNTAINS ABBEY: WATERCOLOUR DRAWING BY PAUL SANDBY MUNN

BREAKING THE CLOD: DRAWING BY J. S. COTMAN, *c.* 1807

SKILL

OVER all the countryside, wherever one goes, indications of techniques are visible to the seeing eye. By technique is meant an exercise of skill acquired by practice and directed to a well foreseen end. It is the name for the action of any of our powers after they have been so improved by training as to perform that action with certainty and success. This is the nature of technique; and, go where one will about the country, one can hardly escape the evidences of its abundant practice.

The metalled roads tell of it well. The deep-rutted by-roads, too, and the winding lanes, preserve through years of neglect the traces of technique in their hedgerows, however tangled; in their ditches, however choked. On the old ruinous field gate, with its lightly-arched, tapering top bar rudely carved on the under side against the tenon, the grey lichen cannot hide the signs of a vitality more marvellous than its own – the intensified vitality of those skilled hands that shaped the timbers. The fields, newly ploughed in straight furrows, or with stubble in long rows, or green lines of wheat just appearing after snow; and the meadows, well rolled and level, or perhaps still wavy from long-forgotten ploughings; and the river banks; and the copses growing up on old 'stamms'; and the woods, thinned out, and full of decayed stumps of felled trees, are all witnesses to the exercise of technical powers, just as are the tools, the farm implements, the waggons and carts, the very horses, and cattle, and sheep. Each detail of country life offers its convincing proof of skill to anyone who cares to look.

GEORGE BOURNE, *Lucy Bettesworth*, 1913

SPRING

Now that the winter's gone, the earth hath lost
Her snow-white robes; and now no more the frost
Candies the grass, or casts an icy cream
Upon the silver lake or crystal stream;
But the warm sun thaws the benumbèd earth,
And makes it tender; gives a second birth
To the dead swallow; wakes in hollow tree
The drowsy cuckoo and the humble-bee.
Now do a choir of chirping minstrels sing,
In triumph to the world, the youthful Spring:
The valleys, hills, and woods, in rich array
Welcome the coming of the longed-for May . . .

THOMAS CAREW, *Poems*, 1640

O KEEN pellucid air! nothing can lurk
Or disavow itself on this bright day;
The small rain-plashes shine from far away,
The tiny emmet glitters at his work;
The bee looks blithe and gay, and as she plies
Her task, and moves and sidles round the cup
Of this spring flower, to drink its honey up,
Her glassy wings, like oars that dip and rise,
Gleam momently. Pure-bosomed, clear of fog,
The long lake glistens, while the glorious beam
Bespangles the wet joints and floating leaves
Of water-plants, whose every point receives
His light; and jellies of the spawning frog,
Unmarked before, like piles of jewels seem!

REV. CHARLES TENNYSON TURNER
Small Tableaux, 1868

136

SUMMER

FAR off the rook, tired by the midday beam,
  Caws lazily this summer afternoon;
  The butterflies, with wandering up and down
O'er flower-bright marsh and meadow, wearied seem;
With vacant gaze, lost in a waking dream,
  We, listless, on the busy insects pore,
  In rapid dance uncertain, darting o'er
The smooth-spread surface of the tepid stream;
The air is slothful, and will scarce convey
  Soft sounds of idle waters to the ear;
  In brightly-dim obscurity appear
The distant hills which skirt the landscape gay;
While restless fancy owns the unnerving sway
  In visions often changed, but nothing clear.

THOMAS DOUBLEDAY, *Sixty-five Sonnets*, 1818

I GAVE a moment to encase my books,
And I was in the sunshine, and my blood
Sprang at its greeting. I was in the fields,
And up around me sprang the larks like rockets
On a jubilee day: – a bank of sand surmounting,
I stepp'd into a wood, with pleasant care,
Opening the twining branches, that imposed
Desirable hindrance: angrily scream'd
A swiftly darting throstle on before me;
Two bees adown the narrow pathway flew,
And a bewilder'd butterfly; I stay'd
To joy in the delicious noise of leaves,

137

In the fresh earthy smells; – I wander'd on
Past the slow-pacing pheasant, and the jay,
Who would not let me leave him, but still follow'd
With his harsh scream.   And now I reach'd an opening,
A short-turf'd lawn, that fenced by silvery stems
Of circling beeches, seem'd a quiet home.
I enter'd; flowingly between the trees
Floated the blackbird's strains; they paused, I paused;
Raising in sympathy to the tranquil heaven
My tranquil thought; like a great eye it shone,
It seem'd to bend in love; I gazed, and gazed;
Its look sank nearer me; I gasp'd, I fell,
Panting to be embraced up by the heaven,
As virgin womanhood for love's caress;
My soul close clung to that far-stretching glory,
'Neath which I reel'd; it stretch'd there undisturb'd
By tower or boundary, and my tranced spirit
Passively drank in its elysian calm.
Oh, blue, blue sky! oh fathomlessly blue sky!
Your motionless band of silvery cloudlets,
Like white swans sleeping on a windless lake,
In happy undesiring repose, – were not
More compass'd by you, more retired within you,
Than I, in that blest time; nor wish, nor thought,
Nor hope, nor grief, found room within my being,
Fill'd with your beautiful presence.

Within the sanctuary of these circling trees,
Thus lay I, slave to the sky; when a white deer
Noiselessly through the intertangled boughs
Did thrust his head; he shrank, and in the forest

Back vanished, most like a silvery cloud.
Retreating, he had shaken on my face
A blown convolvulus; the which upholding
Against the sun, that I might read its veins,
From its recess a crimson-scaled wonder,
A ladybird with richly-spotted wings,
Soar'd through the sunshine. Now from heaven's thraldom
My mind this insect's flight enfranchised;
And being freed to all the things around,
They all impress'd me. Now I heard the partridge
Make the copse echo with his cheerful crow;
Anon my pulsings seem'd to keep the time
Of the cuckoo's music; in the sun's faint streamings.
I watch'd the twinkling bands of tipsy insects;
I watch'd the sun's gold lustre through the leaves,
Illuminating all their make, descend,
As the breeze swerved them into it for a moment,
Letting them drop again. A hundred beauties,
Words will not image, throng'd my echoing soul;
And she from all instinctively did abstract
Their capital feature; life, a massive lyre,
On my proud thought-directed vision rose,
Swinging within its home of boundlessness,
Singing for ever in an Eternal Breeze,
Of whom this landscape, with its gentle beauty,
Was one soft utterance. . . .

EBENEZER JONES, from 'Inactivity'
Studies of Sensation and Event, 1843

AUTUMN

THE rain of a night and a day and a night
Stops at the light
Of this pale choked day. The peering sun
Sees what has been done.
The road under the trees has a border new
Of purple hue
Inside the border of bright thin grass:
For all that has
Been left by November of leaves is torn
From hazel and thorn
And the greater trees. Throughout the copse
No dead leaf drops
On grey grass, green moss, burnt-orange fern,
At the wind's return:
The leaflets out of the ash-tree shed
Are thinly spread
In the road, like little black fish, inlaid,
As if they played.
What hangs from the myriad branches down there
So hard and bare
Is twelve yellow apples lovely to see
On one crab-tree.
And on each twig of every tree in the dell
Uncountable
Crystals both dark and bright of the rain
That begins again.

EDWARD THOMAS, *Last Poems,* 1918

WINTER

THE haze upon the meadow
  Denies the dying year,
For the sun's within it, something bridal
  Is more than dreaming here.
There is no end, no severance,
No moment of deliverance,
  No quietus made,
Though quiet abounds and deliverance moves
  In that sunny shade.

What is winter? A word,
  A figure, a clever guess.
That time-word does not answer to
  This drowsy wakefulness.
The secret stream scorns interval
Though the calendar shouts one from the wall;
  The spirit has no last days;
And death is no more dead than this
  Flower-haunted haze.

EDMUND BLUNDEN
Shells by a Stream, 1944

LANE

A LITTLE lane – the brook runs close beside,
   And spangles in the sunshine, while the fish glide swiftly by;
And hedges leafing with the green springtide;
   From out their greenery the old birds fly,
And chirp and whistle in the morning sun;
   The pilewort glitters 'neath the pale blue sky,
The little robin has its nest begun,
   The grass-green linnets round the bushes fly.
How mild the spring comes in! the daisy buds
   Lift up their golden blossoms to the sky.
How lovely are the pingles and the woods!
   Here a beetle runs – and there a fly
Rests on the arum leaf in bottle-green,
And all the spring in this sweet lane is seen.

JOHN CLARE, *Poems*, 1935
(written *c.* 1850)

           I LOVE to meet
A sudden turn like this, that stops me short,
Extravagantly devious, and invites
Or up the hill or down; then winds again,
By reeling drunkard trod, and all at once
Ends in a green-sward waggon way, that, like
Cathedral aisle completely roofed with branches,
Runs through the wood from top to bottom,
And has at either end a gothic door
Wide open.

REV. JAMES HURDIS, *The Village Curate*, 1788

142

LANDSCAPE WITH COTTAGES: WATERCOLOUR DRAWING BY JOHN CROME

LANDSCAPE IN ESSEX (DETAIL): PAINTING BY IVON HITCHENS, 1946

FOOTPATH

THERE are few footpaths that are new, and those that are old may be drowned or cut to pieces, or may be incorporated (as De Quincey has said) in someone's kitchen, but seem never to die, and the more they are down-trodden the more they flourish. Curiosity as to whether Shakespeare ever started one is idle. They are footprints, perhaps of the immortals. They are vestiges of that older day when this land also 'was in Arcady'. Even today they may be seen, after rising and falling in the fields, to be gathered into that far country again, where hills like clouds and clouds like hills are mingled beneath the white sun of noon.

EDWARD THOMAS, *Horae Solitariae*, 1902

THE secret beauties of Nature are unveiled only to the cross-country walker. Pan would not have appeared to Pheidippides on a road. On the road we never meet the 'moving accidents by flood and field'; the sudden glory of a woodland glade; the open back-door of the old farmhouse sequestered deep in rural solitude; the cow routed up from meditation behind the stone wall as we scale it suddenly; the deep, slow, south-country stream that we must jump, or wander along to find the bridge; the northern torrent of molten peat-hag that we must ford up to the waist, to scramble, glowing warm-cold, up the farther foxglove bank; the autumnal dew on the bracken and the blue straight smoke of the cottage in the still glen at dawn; the rush down the mountain-side, hair flying, stones and grouse rising at our feet; and at the bottom the plunge in the pool below the waterfall, in a place so fair that kings should come from far to bathe therein – yet it is left, year in year out, unvisited save by us and 'troops of stars'.

G. M. TREVELYAN, *Clio, a Muse*, 1913

ASH AND WILLOW

Not of all my eyes see, wandering on the world,
Is anything a milk to the mind so, so sighs deep
Poetry to it, as a tree whose boughs break in the sky.
Say it is ash-boughs: whether on a December day and furled
Fast or they in clammyish lashtender combs creep
Apart wide and new-nestle at heaven most high.
They touch heaven, tabour on it; how their talons sweep
The smouldering enormous winter welkin! May
Mells blue and snow white through them, a fringe and fray
Of greenery: it is old earth's groping towards the steep
    Heaven whom she childs us by.

GERALD MANLEY HOPKINS, *Poems*, 1930
(written *c.* 1885)

And bright and silvery the willows sleep
Over the shady verge – no mad winds tease
Their hoary heads; but quietly they weep
Their sprinkling leaves – half fountains and half trees.

THOMAS HOOD, from 'The Two Swans'
Poems, 1846

BEECH AND YEW

On the north escarpment of the downs, at this point, there are some fine yew groves and woods in the deep combes and hollows and ravine-like clefts in the sides of the hills. The finest of these is on the north side of the great down west of West Dean woods. Here, in the side of the hill, there is an immense basin-shaped combe, its sloping circular sides covered with a dense dark growth of yews, and, under these, the flat bottom of the basin is filled with a beechen wood. Seated on the turf on the rim of this great hollow in the side of the hill, one evening in late January, I had beneath me a scene to make a man's heart glad. I had only just discovered this hidden wood, and it came as a complete surprise; nothing quite like it had I seen before. In summer, when the beeches would appear from above as a floor of deep uniform green, there would not perhaps have been any special beauty in this spot. Winter had given the charm and magical effect it had for me on that evening, when the sun was going down in a cold but very clear sky. For the tall beeches on which I looked down appeared as innumerable white or pale columns standing on a floor of red and russet gold, and white columns and golden floor were all the more beautiful for being seen through the almost cloud-like tracery of innumerable purple and purplish-red or 'murrey'-coloured branchlets. The rich colour of that temple and palace of nature – the golden floor and purple roof – made the wide band of the yew wood seem black by contrast: and above the black yews the smooth turf of the hill-top looked a pale green.

W. H. HUDSON, *Nature in Downland*, 1900

IN THE MEADOWS

Now time stands still, and the meadows lie
Entranced, under a burning sky,
Where cumulus clouds, like ships at anchor,
Seem to pause in their drifting by.

Lazy, alone, I lie in the grass,
Knowing the moment will never pass,
Having as yet no art to embitter
The joy that is with a joy that was.

The blades of grass are a forest of trees,
Where insect-characters dwell at ease.
I watch them on their busy occasions
Coming and going as they please.

And near by, should I choose to look,
In the crystal glaze of a pebbly brook
Other acquaintances live, too little
To be attempted with line and hook.

The sun at his zenith, the earth a-swoon,
Stilled by the brazen gong of noon,
I lie in the grass. I look. I listen.
The warm air murmurs a drowsy tune.

GERALD BULLETT, 'High Noon'
Windows on a Vanished Time, 1955

LTSHIRE PASTORAL: PAINTING BY SIR WILLIAM NICHOLSON, *c.* 1925

Studies for group September (Cornfield, Barley)

STUDIES OF BARLEY: DRAWING BY ALAN REYNOLDS, 1954

CORNFIELD

SUMMER ends now; now, barbarous in beauty, the stooks arise
  Around; up above, what wind-walks! what lovely behaviour
  Of silk-sack clouds! has wilder, wilful-wavier
Meal-drift moulded ever and melted across skies?

I walk, I lift up, I lift up heart, eyes,
  Down all that glory in the heavens to glean our Saviour;
  And, eyes, heart, what looks, what lips yet gave you a
Rapturous love's greeting of realer, of rounder replies?

And the azurous hung hills are his world-wielding shoulder
  Majestic – as a stallion stalwart, very-violet-sweet! –
These things, these things were here and but the beholder
  Wanting; which two when they once meet,
The heart rears wings bold and bolder
  And hurls for him, O half hurls earth for him off under his feet.

GERALD MANLEY HOPKINS, *Poems*, 1930
(written 1877)

BURN

THE midges dance aboon the burn,
  The dews begin to fa',
The partricks down the rushy holm
  Set up their e'ening ca'.
Now loud and clear the blackbird's sang
  Rings through the briery shaw,
While, flitting gay, the swallows play
  Around the castle wa'.

Beneath the golden gloaming sky
  The mavis mends her lay;
The redbreast pours his sweetest strains
  To charm the ling'ring day;
While weary yeldrins seem to wail
  Their little nestlings torn,
The merry wren, frae den to den,
  Gaes jinking through the thorn.

The roses fauld their silken leaves,
  The foxglove shuts its bell,
The honeysuckle and the birk
  Spread fragrance through the dell.
Let others crowd the giddy court
  Of mirth and revelry,
The simple joys that Nature yields
  Are dearer far to me.

ROBERT TANNAHILL, *Poems and Songs*, 1815

BROOK

O DEEP unlovely brooklet, moaning slow
   Thro' moorish fen in utter loneliness!
The partridge cowers beside thy loamy flow
   In pulseful tremor, when with sudden press
The huntsman fluskers thro' the rustled heather.
   In March thy sallow-buds from vermeil shells
Break satin-tinted, downy as the feather
   Of moss-chat that among the purplish bells
Breasts into fresh new life her three unborn.
   The plover hovers o'er thee, uttering clear
And mournful-strange, his human cry forlorn:
   While wearily, alone, and void of cheer
Thou guid'st thy nameless waters from the fen,
To sleep unsunned in an untrampled glen.

DAVID GRAY
The Luggie and Other Poems, 1862

BUTTERFLY

HERE Lucy paused for the blue butterfly –
Blue with the mingled colours of the sky:
Here Lucy paused, and murmured to behold
His fingers long or feelers ringed with gold,
Ebony-ringed like cowboy's switches are,
And touched with sunset and its seraph star.

Frilled round he was, she bade me look, with white;
Over his body blossomed a soft light;
And in his wings a ruddiness remained
Like thunder skies, yet thence his sweet blue gained;
And when he shut his timid wings, then even
His undersides proclaimed a child of heaven,
Flecked with dark eyes, in paly circlets crowned.

Vetches of scarlet vein were legion round;
The speckled orchid grew, wild bean beside;
The aspens like a pebbled water sighed;
When he rose up to feathery fanning flight
And over sweetbriar dancing went from sight.
And here I see him yet, and Lucy's eye
Smiles on him from that day so fast fled by,
And her delight so trembling and so true
Is whispering in my lonely walk anew.

EDMUND BLUNDEN, *English Poems*, 1925

OPLAR HAWK MOTH: ENGRAVING AFTER ELEAZAR ALBIN, 1720

LIVERPOOL DELFT POTTERY DISH, *c.* 1750

BIRD

REPEAT that, repeat,
Cuckoo, bird, and open ear wells, heart-springs,
   delightfully sweet,
With a ballad, with a ballad, a rebound
Off trundled timber and scoops of the hillside ground,
   hollow hollow hollow ground:
The whole landscape flushes on a sudden at a sound.

GERALD MANLEY HOPKINS, *Poems,* 1930
(written *c.* 1880)

UPON this leafy bush
   With thorns and roses in it,
Flutters a thing of light,
   A twittering linnet,
And all the throbbing world
   Of dew and sun and air
By this small parcel of life
   Is made more fair:
As if each bramble-spray
   And mounded gold-wreathed furze,
Harebell and little thyme,
   Were only hers;
As if this beauty and grace
   Did to one bird belong,
And, at a flutter of wing,
   Might vanish in song.

WALTER DE LA MARE, *Motley,* 1918

157

SOUNDS

ON a morning early in May it was raining, quietly, luxuriously, with a continuous soothing shattering-down of warm drops. In the doorway of the little tool-shed I stood listening – listening to the gentle murmur on the roof, on the long fresh grass of a small orchard plot, and on the young leaves of the plum and the blossoming apple which made the daylight greener by half veiling the sky.

Beside and beyond these trees were lilacs, purpling for bloom, small hazels, young elms in a hedgerow – all fair with new greenness; and farther on, glimpses of cottage roof against the newly-dug garden-ground of the steep hillside. Above the half-diaphanous green tracery of the trees, cool delicious cloud, 'dropping fatness', darkened where it sagged nearer to the earth. . . .

I ought to have been busy, yet I stood and listened; for the earth seemed busy too, but in a softened way, managing its many businesses beautifully. The air seemed melting into numberless liquid sounds. Quite near – not three trees off – there was a nightingale nonchalantly babbling; from the neighbourhood of the cottage came, penetrating, the bleating of a newly-born goat; while in the orchard just before me Bettesworth stooped over a zinc pail, which, as he scrubbed it, gave out a low metallic note. Then there were three undertones or backgrounds of sound, that of the soft-falling rain being one of them. Another, which diapered the rain-noise just as the young leaves showed their diaper-work against the clouds, was the all but unnoticed singing of larks, high up in the wet. Lastly, to give the final note of mellowness, of flavoured richness to the morning, I could hear through the distance which globed and softened it a frequent 'Cuckoo, cuckoo'. The sound came and died away, as if the rain had dissolved it, and came again, and again was lost.

GEORGE BOURNE, *Memoirs of a Surrey Labourer*, 1907

SCENTS

TO-DAY I think
Only with scents, – scents dead leaves yield,
And bracken, and wild carrot's seed,
And the square mustard field;

Odours that rise
When the spade wounds the root of tree,
Rose, currant, raspberry, or goutweed,
Rhubarb or celery;

The smoke's smell, too,
Flowing from where a bonfire burns
The dead, the waste, the dangerous,
And all to sweetness turns.

It is enough
To smell, to crumble the dark earth,
While the robin sings over again
Sad songs of Autumn mirth.

EDWARD THOMAS, *Last Poems*, 1918

THE WIND

I LOVE the fitful gust that shakes
   The casement all the day,
And from the mossy elm tree takes
   The faded leaves away,
Twirling them by the window pane
With thousand others down the lane.

I love to see the shaking twig
   Dance till the shut of eve,
The sparrow on the cottage rig,
   Whose chirp would make believe
That spring was just now flirting by
In summer's lap with flowers to lie.

I love to see the cottage smoke
   Curl upwards through the trees,
The pigeons nestled round the cote
   On November days like these;
The cock upon the dunghill crowing,
The mill-sails on the heath a-going.

The feather from the raven's breast,
   Falls on the stubble lea;
The acorns near the old crow's nest
   Drop pattering down the tree;
The grunting pigs, that wait for all,
Scramble and hurry where they fall.

JOHN CLARE, *Poems*, 1920 (written *c.* 1850)

AND THE RAIN

FROM the sad eaves the drip-drop of the rain!
The water washing at the latchel door;
A slow step plashing by upon the moor!
A single bleat far from the famished fold:
The clicking of an embered hearth and cold;
The rainy Robin tic-tac at the pane.

'So as it is with thee
Is it with me,
So as it is and it used not to be,
With thee used not to be,
Nor me.'
So singeth Robin on the willow tree,
The rainy Robin tic-tac at the pane.

Here in this breast all day
The fire is dim and low,
Within I care not to stay,
Without I care not to go.

A sadness ever sings
Of unforgotten things,
And the bird of love is patting at the pane;
But the wintry water deepens at the door,
And a step is plashing by upon the moor,
Into the dark upon the darkening moor,
And alas, alas, the drip-drop of the rain!

SYDNEY DOBELL
England in Time of War, 1856

161

CRICKETERS on village greens, hay-makers in the evening sunshine, small boats that sail before the wind – all these create in me the illusion of Happiness, as if a land of cloudless pleasure, a piece of the old Golden World, were hidden, not (as poets have fancied) in far seas or beyond inaccessible mountains, but here close at hand, if one could find it, in some undiscoverable valley. Certain grassy lanes seem to lead through the copses thither; the wild pigeons talk of it behind the woods.

LOGAN PEARSALL SMITH, *Trivia*, 1918

SPORTING PRINT

It may be said that there are things of more importance than striking a ball against a wall – there are things indeed which make more noise and do as little good, such as making war . . .

WILLIAM HAZLITT

WIND thy horn, my hunter boy,
  And leave thy lute's inglorious sighs;
Hunting is the hero's joy,
  Till war his nobler game supplies.

THOMAS MOORE, *Poetical Works*, 1840

ENJOY thy streame, O harmless fish;
And when an angler, for his dish,
  Through gluttony's vile sin,
Attempts, a wretch, to pull thee out,
God give thee strength, O gentel trout,
  To pull the raskall in!

JOHN WOLCOT, *Works*, 1801

I'D rather drive an engine than
Be a little gentleman;
I'd rather go shunting and hooting
Than hunting and shooting.

DANIEL PETTIWARD, *Truly Rural*, 1939

EXERCISE

... COME, country Goddess, come; nor thou suffice,
But bring thy mountain-sister, Exercise,
Call'd by thy lively voice, she turns her pace,
Her winding horn proclaims the finish'd chace;
She mounts the rocks, she skims the level plain,
Dogs, hawks, and horses, crowd her early train;
Her hardy face repels the tanning wind,
And lines and meshes loosely float behind.
All these as means of toil the feeble see,
But these are helps to pleasure join'd with thee,
   Let Sloth lie soft'ning till high noon in down,
Or lolling fan her in the sultry town,
Unnerv'd with rest; and turn her own disease,
Or foster others in luxurious ease:
I mount the courser, call the deep-mouth'd hounds,
The fox unkennell'd flies to covert grounds;
I lead where stags thro' tangled thickets tread,
And shake the saplings with their branching head;
I make the faulcons wing their airy way,
And soar to seize, or stooping strike their prey;
To snare the fish I fix the luring bait;
To wound the fowl I load the gun with fate.
'Tis thus thro' change of exercise I range,
And strength and pleasure rise from ev'ry change. ...

DR. THOMAS PARNELL, from 'Health, An Eclogue'
Poems on Several Occasions, 1722

THE BRADFORD TABLE CARPET (DETAIL): ELIZABETHAN EMBROIDERY

THE TACKLE: SCULPTURE BY PETER L. PERI, 1953

CONFLICT AND ART

THIRTY-FIVE thousand men and boys have just seen what most of them called 't'United' play Bolton Wanderers. . . . To say that these men paid their shillings to watch twenty-two hirelings kick a ball is merely to say that a violin is wood and catgut, that Hamlet is so much paper and ink.

For a shilling the Bruddersford United A.F.C. offered you Conflict and Art; it turned you into a critic, happy in your judgment of fine points, ready in a second to estimate the worth of a well-judged pass, a run down the touch line, a lightning shot, a clearance kick by back or goalkeeper; it turned you into a partisan, holding your breath when the ball came sailing into your own goalmouth, ecstatic when your forwards raced away towards the opposite goal, elated, downcast, bitter, triumphant by turns at the fortunes of your side, watching a ball shape Iliads and Odysseys for you; and what is more, it turned you into a member of a new community, all brothers together for an hour and a half, for not only have you escaped from the clanking machinery of this lesser life, from work, wages, rent, doles, sick pay, insurance cards, nagging wives, ailing children, bad bosses, idle workmen, but you had escaped with most of your mates and your neighbours, with half the town, and there you were, cheering together, thumping one another on the shoulders, swopping judgments like lords of the earth, having pushed your way through a turnstile into another and altogether more splendid kind of life, hurtling with Conflict and yet passionate and beautiful in its Art. Moreover, it offered you more than a shilling's worth of material for talk during the rest of the week. A man who had missed the last home match of 't'United' had to enter social life on tiptoe in Bruddersford.

J. B. PRIESTLEY, The Good Companions, 1929

THE WORLD'S THE JACK

HERE's your right ground: wag gently o'er this black;
  'Tis a short cast; y're quickly at the Jack;
Rub, rub an inch or two; two crowns to one
  On this bowl's side; blow wind; 'tis fairly thrown.
The next bowl's worse that comes; come, bowl away;
  Mammon, you know the ground untutored, play;
Your last was gone; a yard of strength, well spared,
  Had touched the block; your hand is still too hard.
Brave pastime, Readers, to consume that day,
  Which, without pastime, flies too swift away:
See how they labour; as if day and night
  Were both too short to serve their loose delight;
See how their curved bodies wreathe and screw
  Such antic shapes as Proteus never knew;
One raps an oath; another deals a curse;
  He never better bowled; this, never worse:
One rubs his itchless elbow, shrugs, and laughs;
  The tother bends his beetle-brows, and chaffs,
Sometime they whoop; sometimes their Stygian cries
  Send their Black-Santos to the blushing skies;
Thus, mingling humours in a mad confusion,
  They make bad premises, and worse conclusion:
But where's the palm that fortune's hand allows
  To bless the victor's honourable brows?
Come, Reader, come; I'll light thine eye the way
  To view the prize, the while the gamesters play. . . .

FRANCIS QUARLES, *Emblems*, 1635

SPLENDOUR ON THE LINKS

How straight it flew, how long it flew,
    It clear'd the rutty track
And soaring, disappeared from view
    Beyond the bunker's back –
A glorious, sailing, bounding drive
That made me glad I was alive.

And down the fairway, far along
    It glowed a lonely white;
I played an iron sure and strong
    And clipp'd it out of sight,
And spite of grassy banks between
I knew I'd find it on the green.

And so I did. It lay content
    Two paces from the pin;
A steady putt and then it went
    Oh, most securely in.
The very turf rejoiced to see
That quite unprecedented three.

Ah! seaweed smells from sandy caves
    And thyme and mist in whiffs,
In-coming tide, Atlantic waves
    Slapping the sunny cliffs,
Lark song and sea sounds in the air
And splendour, splendour everywhere.

JOHN BETJEMAN, *A Few Late Chrysanthemums*, 1954

169

THE MOTIVE ORB

In winter, too, when hoary frosts o'erspread
The verdant turf, and naked lay the mead,
The vigorous youth commence the sportive war,
And, armed with lead, their jointed clubs prepare:
The timber curve to leathern orbs apply,
Compact, elastic, to pervade the sky:
These to the distant hole direct they drive;
They claim the stakes who thither first arrive.
Intent his ball the eager gamester eyes,
His muscles strains, and various postures tries,
Th' impelling blow to strike with greater force,
And shape the motive orb's projectile course.
If with due strength the weighty engine fall,
Discharged obliquely, and impinge the ball,
It winding mounts aloft, and sings in air;
And wondering crowds the gamester's skill declare.
But when some luckless wayward stroke descends,
Whose force the ball in running quickly spends,
The foes triùmph, the club is cursed in vain;
Spectators scoff, and ev'n allies complain,
Thus still success is followed with applause;
But ah! how few espouse a vanquished cause!

JAMES ARBUCKLE, *Glotta*, 1721

WILLIAM ST CLAIR OF ROSLIN: PAINTING BY SIR GEORGE CHALMERS, *c.* 1776

THE CRICKET MATCH: PAINTING BY SPENCER FREDERICK GORE, 1909

CEREMONY IN SUNSHINE

THE occasion in most parts of the world is sunshine, and the time is youth – for these seniors round you when they slipped away from their offices dropped their burden of age, and the boys and girls are all excitement and dream. The ceremony we witness is graceful, and unless some unfortunate batsman plays a ball with his ear or his ribs it exacts no sacrifice; it requires moreover no thesis on our part, no lopping and planing of the mind's branchings and twigs so as to produce a blunt 'opinion', or article of belief. There will be triumphs of individuals and triumphs of bodies corporate – and there will be none. If a cat chooses to take a walk out into the arena, it will be an incident as memorable as the marvellous technical luxuries we are given; and if one of the boys squeezing under the ropes has the luck to have the ball bounce into his hands and throw it in to the great man in flannels who just failed to overhaul it – the boy knows who he is, as much as he knows who rules Russia – we share his thrill. The next free day we get, perhaps we shall dig the allotment, or saunter in a flower-garden, or climb with the cloud-shadows or float on the river with the moorhens; but this day we give to society without society's strain and struggle. The faces about us are easy. There are good notes in the voices, as when some fine old farmer recognizes a thirsty companion of the bat and pads after an interval of many years. . . . And here they can converse of matters that rise fairly over the red-lit tumults and nightmares of the world since last they met: 'Now *she* married young Tim Kettle the piano-tuner,' 'That never was a house to live in,' 'They tell me there's a proposal to open up that old channel between Sammons's and the Bellmouth Bend,' 'The offertory has been slightly better lately.' If only the clock would not insist on behaving much like clocks elsewhere, here would be eternity, and the cluster of oaks at the corner of the ground would be a green temple for ever at the entry to so unworldly a place.

But then, the heroes themselves! No men ever wear their laurels more simply. They have more than skill; they have the spirit of the game, of the mystery, and I have watched them often with a yearning that their composure might extend to the contentious world beyond their greensward. We hear occasionally of a strife between even them, and we are glad when the mutterings die away, for it is so little like the prevailing serenity with which they pursue their art. In success, in unsuccess they are equable, and humorous, and sympathetic. This courtesy of theirs, if one could put it into words, might convert the most obstinate enemies of cricket; and I have never ceased to feel a little unsatisfied when, off the field, the press tells me something of one or other of them which stamps them as frail mortals after all. But that is 'off the field', outside the charmed circle, outside their especial destiny; and on other days or hours than those when the complete secret of cricket unites them and us in a very perfect gentle island of innocence.

EDMUND BLUNDEN, *Cricket Country*, 1944

ON Sunday morning early, we saw a crowd going up the street, and immediately perceived that in the centre of it were the Sussex Cricketers, just arrived by the London coach, and going to an inn kept by one of the Nottingham cricketers. . . .

On Monday morning we set off to the cricket-ground, which lies about a mile from the town, in the Forest, as it is still called, though not a tree is left upon it – a long, furzy common, crowned at the top by about twenty windmills, and descending in a steep slope to a fine level, round which the race-course runs. Within the race-course lies the cricket-ground, which was enclosed at each end with booths; and all up the forest hill were scattered booths, and tents with flags flying, fires burning, pots boiling, ale-barrels standing, and asses, carts and people bringing still more good things. There were plenty of apple and ginger-beer stalls; and lads going round with nuts and with waggish looks, crying 'nuts, lads! nuts, lads!' . . .

Standing on the farther side of the cricket ground, it gave me the most vivid idea possible, of an amphitheatre filled with people. In fact, it was an amphitheatre. Along each side of the ground ran a bank sloping down to it, and it, and the booths and tents at the ends were occupied with a dense mass of people, all as silent as the ground beneath them; and all up the hill were groups, and on the race-stand an eager, forward leaning throng. There were said to be twenty thousand people, all hushed as death, except when some exploit of the players produced a thunder of applause. The playing was beautiful. Mr. Ward, late member of parliament for London, a great cricket player, came from the Isle of Wight to see the game, and declared himself highly delighted. But nothing was so beautiful as the sudden shout, the rush and breaking up of the crowd when the last decisive match was gained. To see the scorers suddenly snatch up their chairs, and run off with them towards the players' tent; to see the bat of Bart Goode, the batsman on whom the fate of the game depended, spinning up in the air, where he had sent it in the ecstasy of the moment; and the crowd, that the instant before was fixed and silent as the world itself, spreading all over the green space where the white figures of the players had till then been so gravely and apparently calmly contending – spreading with a murmur as of the sea; and over their heads, amid the deafening clamour and confusion, the carrier-pigeon with a red ribbon tied to its tail, the signal of loss, beating round and round as to ascertain its precise position, and then flying off to bear the tidings to Brighton – it was a beautiful sight, and one that the most sedate person must have delighted to see.

WILLIAM HOWITT, *The Rural Life of England*, 1838

THE ARCHERY MEETING

THE Archery meeting is fixed for the third;
The fuss that it causes is truly absurd;
I've bought summer bonnets for Rosa and Bess,
And now I must buy each an archery dress!
Without a green suit they would blush to be seen,
And poor little Rosa looks horrid in green!

Poor fat little Rosa! she's shooting all day!
She sends forth an arrow expertly they say;
But 'tis terrible when with exertion she warms,
And she seems to be getting such muscular arms;
And if she should hit, 'twere as well if she missed,
Prize bracelets could never be clasped on her wrist!

Dear Bess with her elegant figure and face,
Looks quite a Diana, the queen of the place;
But as for the shooting – she never takes aim;
She talks so, and laughs so! the beaux are to blame;
She dotes on flirtation – but oh! by-the-bye,
'Twas awkward her shooting out Mrs. Flint's eye. . . .

THOMAS HAYNES BAYLY
Songs, Ballads, and Other Poems, 1844

THE FAIR TOXOPHILITES: PAINTING BY W. P. FRITH, R.A., 1872

OLD FORD PRINTED COTTON CURTAIN (DETAIL), 1769

ON A BANK AS I SATE A-FISHING

AND now all Nature seem'd in love;
The lusty sap began to move;
New juice did stir th' embracing vines;
And birds had drawn their Valentines:
The jealous trout, that low did lie,
Rose at a well-dissembled flie:
There stood my friend, with patient skill
Attending of his trembling quill.
Already were the eaves possest
With the swift pilgrims' daubèd nest.
The groves already did rejoice
In Philomel's triumphing voice.
The showers were short, the weather mild,
The morning fresh, the evening smil'd.
The fields and gardens were beset
With tulip, crocus, violet.
And now, though late, the modest rose
Did more than half a blush disclose.
Thus all looked gay, all full of cheer,
To welcome the new-liveried year.

SIR HENRY WOTTON
Reliquiae Wottonianæ, 1651

WATERY WILES

WHEN April strews the woods with primrose flowers,
When oft the day is dimmed with hovering showers,
When cuckoo birds repeat th' unchanging song,
And muddy rivers sluggish steal along, –
The watery wiles now long disused prepare,
Unloose the ravelled line with patient care,
Fix well the hook, then dip the sapless wand,
And throw the line athwart with waving hand.
Slowly it glides down with the dusky flood,
Bearing along the fatal treacherous food,
It sinks – it sinks again – but do not pull;
'Tis but the nibbling of some sportive fool;
Wait cautious till the floating signal dive;
Now gently pull, O do not rashly strive;
The slender wand to every motion bends,
And yielding, in a drooping crescent ends;
Soon in the bank the struggling captive lies,
Then in the wicker prison gasping dies.

But if thy skill such humble sport deride,
Wait until when the swollen streams subside,
Till when the swallows skim along the flood
And flitting zig-zag catch the insect brood.
O'er night the mimic flies arrange with care,
The brown, the gray, the gilded, and the fair.
With earliest dawn up from thy slumbers spring,
Ere yet the morning birds begin to sing:
And O leave not behind th' unweeting boy,
Nor cheat him dreaming of the promised joy;

Go rouse him gently, see him sleeping smile,
Then, if thou canst, his wakening hopes beguile:
Thy steps he'll follow, grateful and submiss,
Study thy looks, and fear to do amiss.
But feigning angry mien, and wrathful tone,
Command the rambling spaniel to be gone;
Then lightly skiff along the dewy plain,
Until the misty river's side you gain.
If there success you wish, observe this rule, –
Where ends the stream and where begins the pool,
Let the winged lure among the eddies play
And dancing round delude the speckled prey.
Beware – be not impatiently rash,
Nor fretfully the harmless surface lash;
The limber line with wary motion throw,
Let it fall gently like a flake of snow,
Which silent melts as on the stream it lights
And with the watery element unites:
And still be mindful of the heedless eye
Of the small wight who playful sitteth nigh.
So shall your arts a noble prize delude,
So the huge trout shall snatch the seeming food.
See how he shoots along stretching the line:
Indulge his way: do not his force confine.
Fainter and fainter efforts still are tried,
Till on the stream floats his enamelled side;
Pulled slow ashore, he pants with frequent gasp,
And dyes the little hands that scarce around him clasp.

REV. JAMES GRAHAME
Poems, in English, Scotch, and Latin, 1794

THE TAKING OF THE SALMON

... A BIRR! a whirr! the salmon's out
   Far on the rushing river,
He storms a stream with edge of might,
And like a brandished sword of light,
Rolls flashing o'er the surges white,
   A desperate endeavour!
Hark to the music of the reel!
   The fitful and the grating;
It pants along the breathless wheel,
   Now hurried, now abating. . . .

A birr! a whirr! the salmon's up!
   Give line, give line and measure;
And now he turns, keep down a'head,
And lead him as a child is led,
   And land him at your leisure.
Hark to the music of the reel!
   'Tis welcome, it is glorious;
It wanders round the exultant wheel,
   Returning and victorious. . . .

THOMAS TOD STODDART, *An Angler's Rambles,* 1866

SALMON FISHING IN THE HIGHLANDS: WALLPAPER PATTERN, *c.* 1870

GIMCRACK AT NEWMARKET: PAINTING BY GEORGE STUBBS, A.R.A., *c.* 1765

BELVOIR HOUNDS WALKING OUT IN THE PARK: PAINTING BY SIR ALFRED MUNNINGS, P.P.R.A., 1920–21

AT THE DAWNING OF DAY

THE grey eye of morning was dear to my youth,
    When I sprang like the roe from my bed,
With the glow of the passions, the feelings of truth,
    And the light hand of Time on my head.

For then 'twas my maxim through life to be free,
    And to sport my short moments away;
The cry of the hounds was the music for me,
    My glory – the dawn of the day.

In yellow-leaved autumn the haze of the morn
    Gave promise of rapture to come;
Then melody woke in the sound of the horn,
    As we cheer'd the old fox from his home;

The breeze and the shout met the sun's early beam,
    With the village response in full play;
All vigour, my steed leap'd the fence or the stream,
    And was foremost at dawn of the day.

The well-tuned view-halloo that shook the green wood,
    And arrested the ploughman's gay song,
Gave nerve to the hunters, and fire to the blood
    Of the hounds, as they bounded along.

And shall I relinquish this joy of my heart
    While years with my strength roll away?
Hark! the horn – bring my horse – see, they're ready to start!
    Tally-o! at the dawning of day.

ROBERT BLOOMFIELD, *Remains*, 1824

HUNTER'S SONG

Now bonny Bay
In his foam waxeth grey,
Dapple Grey waxeth bay in his blood;
White Lily stops
With the scent in her chops,
And Black Lady makes it good.
Poor silly Wat
In this wretched state
Forgets these delights for to hear;
Nimbly she bounds
From the cry of the hounds
And the music of their career.

Hills with the heat
Of the gallopers sweat,
Reviving their frozen tops;
Dales' purple flowers
They spring from the showers
That down from the rowels drops;
Swains their repast,
And strangers their haste
Neglect when the horns they do hear;
To see a fleet
Pack of hounds in a sheet,
And the hunter in his career. . . .

WILLIAM BASSE, in *Sportive Wit*, 1656
(written *c.* 1627)

A CURE FOR THE SPLEEN

Hunting I reckon very good
To brace the nerves, and stir the blood;
But after no field-honours itch
Achiev'd by leaping hedge and ditch.
While Spleen lies soft relax'd in bed,
Or o'er coal-fire inclines the head,
Hygeia's sons with hound and horn
And jovial cry awake the morn:
These see her from the dusky plight,
Smear'd by th' embraces of the night,
With roral wash redeem her face
And prove herself of Titan's race,
And mounting in loose robes the skies,
Shed light and fragrance, as she flies.
Then horse and hound fierce joy display,
Exulting at the Hark-away,
And in pursuit o'er tainted ground
From lungs robust field-notes resound.
Then as St. George the dragon slew,
Spleen pierc'd, trod down, and dying view,
While all their spirits are on wing,
And woods, and hills, and valleys ring.

MATTHEW GREEN, *The Spleen*, 1737

189

THE OLD ENGLISH SQUIRE

HE kept a stud of racers 'twas his joy to see them run,
And his sideboards were well covered with the gold cups they had
  won,
To the town he represented every year he gave a plate,
And to the course, in coach and six, he always came in state
Six goodly nags they were, though very fat and slow,
Their manes were decked with ribbons, and their flowing tails also;
His lady sat beside him tall and upright as a wand
And the people loudly cheered him on alighting at the stand.

He kept a pack of fox hounds of pure old English breed;
Most musical and staunch they were, but not much famed for speed;
His hunters were enduring, and could go a decent pace;
To suit his hounds he bred them, not to run a steeple-chase;
He boldly went at hedge or gate nor stop't at ditch or brook,
And many a Melton Mowbray swell might shy the leap he took,
'Twas a pleasant sight to see him through a bull find make a gap,
With a pig-tail like a drum stick cocking out behind his hat.

On the first day of September, as the season still came round,
With his pointers in the stubble he was always to be found,
Though his gun was like a musket, an old fashioned flint and steel,
Wide muzzled and a kicker, she was heavy in the heel,
Yet birds, they being plentiful, he brought down many a brace,
And if he found them sitting why he show'd them little grace,
Few thought of shooting flying about fifty years ago,
'Kill when you can' was then the word, and truest shooting low . . .

NINETEENTH-CENTURY BALLAD

190

SPORTSMAN AND HIS SON: PAINTING BY FRANCIS WHEATLEY

DERBY PORCELAIN GROUP, c. 1750

THE SENTIMENTAL SPORTSMAN

THE bosom of Earth is all covered with leaves,
    And the honours of Autumn decay:
Brown Ceres no longer exhibits her sheaves
    To the silver-eyed Monarch of Day.
With the murdering gun hills and valleys resound
    And the swains through the coppices rove:
The partridges bleed on the arable ground,
    And the pheasants lie dead in the grove.

To others such barbarous sport I resign,
    And repose in my Florimel's arms:
My fair one, O come, let me call thee but mine,
    And I'll worship the sun of thy charms!
O come, while the coats of the hedges look green
    Ere the swallows relinquish the mead,
Ere Winter approaches with horrible mien,
    When the flower gives place to the weed . . .

WILLIAM WOTY, *The Shrubs of Parnassus*, 1760

THE GROUSE SHOOTER'S CALL

... SEE! through the gloaming
  The young Morn is coming,
Like a bridal veil round her the silver mist curled,
  Deep as the ruby's rays,
  Bright as the sapphire's blaze,
The banner of day in the East is unfurled.

  The red grouse is scattering
  Dews from his golden wing
Gemmed with the radiance that heralds the day;
  Peace in our Highland vales,
  Health on our mountain gales –
Who would not hie to the Moorlands away!

  Far from the haunts of man
  Mark the grey Ptarmigan,
Seek the lone Moor cock, the pride of our dells.
  Birds of the wilderness!
  Here is their resting place,
Mid the brown heath where the mountain-roe dwells.

  Come then! the heather bloom
  Woos with its wild perfume,
Fragrant and blithsome thy welcome shall be;
  Gaily the fountain sheen,
  Leaps from the mountain green –
Come to our home of the Moorland and lea!

J. W. C., *The Sporting Magazine*, August 1834

194

LEADEN DEATH

SEE! from the brake the whirring pheasant springs,
And mounts exulting on triumphant wings.
Short is his joy; he feels the fiery wound,
Flutters in blood, and panting beats the ground.
Ah! what avail his glossy, varying dyes,
His purple crest, and scarlet-circled eyes,
The vivid green his shining plumes unfold,
His painted wings, and breast that flames with gold?
    Nor yet, when moist Arcturus clouds the sky
The woods and fields their pleasing toils deny.
To plains with well-breath'd beagles we repair,
And trace the mazes of the circling hare.
(Beasts, urg'd by us, their fellow beasts pursue,
And learn of man each other to undo.)
With slaught'ring guns th' unweary'd fowler roves,
When frosts have whiten'd all the naked groves;
Where doves in flocks the leafless trees o'ershade,
And lonely woodcocks haunt the wat'ry glade.
He lifts the tube, and levels with his eye;
Strait a short thunder breaks the frozen sky.
Oft, as in airy rings they skim the heath,
The clam'rous lapwings feel the leaden death;
Oft, as the mounting larks their notes prepare,
They fall, and leave their little lives in air.

ALEXANDER POPE, *Windsor Forest*, 1713

LOVE ON ICE

THE last rose-petal of the sunset's rose
Falls in the further West and faintly glows,
One thought of fire in a world of snows.

She turns, I turn with her. The level rays
Of the low Moon half veiled in opal haze
With rose-white magic light the Eastward ways.

She flies, I follow. Through the glimmering plain
We speed in silence. When I strive to gain
Her side, she holds me back. Wild hopes and vain!

She flies, I follow. Thus her power I own
That am her poor, obsequious shadow grown –
For still I touch her, still I'm left alone!

She flies, I follow. Though her finger-tips
Are all I hold, yet at her unseen lips
My soul flits on before, and bee-like sips.

She flies, I follow. Hear the dulcet chime
Of steel on ice that marks the magic time,
And breaks the rhythmic silence as with rhyme!

She trips, she falls. I hold her in a trice
And colder were her lips than Northern ice,
But warmer was my kiss than Southern skies.

E. B. OSBORN, in Sporting Verse, 1930

ING LOVERS: AQUATINT AFTER ADAM BUCK, 1800

GARDEN SCENE: EARLY EIGHTEENTH-CENTURY EMBROIDERED PICTURE

FLOWER PIECE

HERE in this sequestered close
Bloom the hyacinth and rose;
Here beside the modest stock
Flaunts the flaring hollyhock;
Here, without a pang, one sees
Ranks, conditions, and degrees.

All the seasons run their race
In this quiet resting-place;
Peach and apricot and fig
Here will ripen and grow big;
Here is store and overplus, –
More had not Alcinoüs!

Here, in alleys cool and green,
Far ahead the thrush is seen;
Here along the southern wall
Keeps the bee his festival;
All is quiet else – afar
Sounds of toil and turmoil are.

Here be shadows large and long;
Here be spaces meet for song;
Grant, O garden-god, that I,
Now that none profane is nigh,
Now that mood and moment please,
Find the fair Pierides!

AUSTIN DOBSON
At the Sign of the Lyre, 1885

A MEMORY OF FLOWERS

WHEN I was quite a boy, my father used to take me to the Montpelier Tea-gardens at Walworth. Do I go there now? No; the place is deserted, and its borders and its beds o'erturned. Is there, then, nothing that can

'Bring back the hour
Of glory in the grass, of splendour in the flower?'

Oh! yes. I unlock the casket of memory, and draw back the warders of the brain; and there this scene of my infant wanderings still lives unfaded, or with fresher dyes. A new sense comes upon me, as in a dream; a richer perfume, brighter colours start out; my eyes dazzle; my heart heaves with its new load of bliss, and I am a child again. My sensations are all glossy, spruce, voluptuous, and fine: they wear a candied coat, and are in holiday trim. I see the beds of larkspur with purple eyes; tall holy-oaks, red and yellow; the broad sun-flowers, caked in gold, with bees buzzing round them; wildernesses of pinks, and hot-glowing pionies; poppies run to seed; the sugared lily, and faint mignionette, all ranged in order, and as thick as they can grow; the box-tree borders; the gravel-walks, the painted alcove, the confectionary, the clotted cream: – I think I see them now with sparkling looks; or have they vanished while I have been writing this description of them? No matter; they will return again when I least think of them. All that I have observed since, of flowers and plants, and grass-plots, and of suburb delights, seems, to me, borrowed from 'that first garden of my innocence' – to be slips and scions stolen from that bed of memory.

WILLIAM HAZLITT, from 'Why Distant Objects Please'
Table Talk, 1822

KEW

FROM the oval-shaped flower-bed there rose perhaps a hundred stalks spreading into heart-shaped or tongue-shaped leaves half way up and unfurling at the tip red or blue or yellow petals marked with spots of colour raised upon the surface; and from the red, blue, or yellow gloom of the throat emerged a straight bar, rough with gold dust, and slightly clubbed at the end. The petals were voluminous enough to be stirred by the summer breeze, and when they moved the red, blue, and yellow lights passed one over the other, staining an inch of the brown earth beneath with a spot of the most intricate colour. The light fell either upon the smooth grey black of a pebble, or the shell of a snail with its brown circular veins, or, falling into a rain-drop, it expanded with such intensity of red, blue, and yellow the thin walls of water that one expected them to burst, and disappear. Instead the drop was left in a second silver grey once more, and the light now settled upon the flesh of a leaf, revealing the branching thread of fibre beneath the surface, and again it moved on and spread its illumination in the vast green spaces beneath the dome of the heart-shaped and tongue-shaped leaves. Then the breeze stirred rather more briskly overhead, and the colour was flashed into the air above, into the eyes of the men and the women who walk in Kew Gardens in July.

VIRGINIA WOOLF, *Kew Gardens*, 1927

NATURE

Not Iris in her pride and bravery
Adorns her arch with such variety;
Nor doth the Milk-white Way, in frosty night,
Appear so fair and beautiful in sight
As do these fields and groves and sweeter bowers,
Bestrewed and decked with parti-coloured flowers.
Along the babbling brooks and silver glide,
That at the bottom doth in silence slide:
The watery flowers and lilies on the banks,
Like blazing comets, burgeon all in ranks
Under the hawthorn and the poplar tree
Where sacred Phoebe may delight to be.
The primrose and the purple hyacinth,
The dainty violet and wholesome minth,
The double daisy and the cowslip, queen
Of summer flowers, do o'erpeer the green.
All round the valley, as ye pass,
Ye may not see, for peeping flowers, the grass.

GEORGE PEELE
The Arraignment of Paris, 1584

ART

In what follows, Art sits triumphant, and bids fair for a Co-rivalship with Nature. *Chatsworth*, like a Sun in an hazy Air, adds Lustre to those Dusky Mountains, and attracts a general Congress to be Spectators of its Wonders: . . . The Gardens, very delightful, pleasant and stately, adorn'd with exquisite Water Works; the First we observe is *Neptune* with his Sea-Nymphs from whence, by the turning of a Cock, immediately issue forth several Columns of Water, which seem'd to fall upon Sea-Weeds: Not far from this is another Pond, where Sea-Horses continually rowl; and near to this stands a Tree, composed of Copper, which exactly resembles a Willow; by the turning of a Cock each leaf distils continually Drops of Water, and lively represents a Shower of Rain: From this we pass'd by a Grove of Cypress, upon an Ascent, and came to a Cascade, at the top of which stand Two Sea-Nymphs with each a Jarr under the arm; the Water falling thence upon a Cascade, whilst they seem to squeeze the Vessels, produces a loud rumbling Noise, like what we may imagine of the *Egyptian* or *Indian Cataracts*: At the bottom of the Cascade there is another Pond in which is an Artificial Rose, by turning of a Cock the Water ascends through it, and hangs suspended in the Air in the Figure of that Flower: There is another Pond, wherein is Mercury pointing at the Gods and throwing up Water; besides, there are several Statues of Gladiators, with the Muscles of the Body very lively display'd in their different postures: The Pile is not yet finish'd, but will assuredly be a very compleat and magnificent structure, and worthy of so illustrious a Family.

DR. CHARLES LEIGH
Natural History of Lancashire, Cheshire and the Peak, 1700

PLEASURE GROUND

Oh, let me wander here
Year after year
Among these formal flowers,
These terraces, these towers,
These tins and things that float
Freely along this moat,
And let me feel at ease
With these expansive trees,
Especially this cedar on supports
That flanks all seven tennis courts!
Oh, let me turn
Towards this nettle-bearing urn
And to these damp full-blown
Old gods and goddesses in stone
That like to pose
Stiffly beside the silken rose,
To dangle grapes before their loves
And aim their discuses at doves
Or at the suave peacocks
Fashioned in yew and box!
Lead me towards this crumbling seat
With lions' feet,
Cluttered with crests
And sparrows' nests,
Or let me travel
Over the well-raked gravel
Beyond brief bridges and still streams
And aptly chosen colour-schemes
And slowly make
My way towards the laundry and the lake,

The dairy, the gazebo and the sheds
Stuffed with ex-cupids and brooms' heads.
Let me pursue these endless drives
And find at length beehives
Jostling for room
Among the onions of the seventh groom;
Guide me to grapes
And massive melons in three shapes;
Lead me to vegetables
And sounds of stamping in the stables,
Wet noses at the kennel bars
And sober stately motor cars. . . .
Somewhere the old night-watchman sleeps
And there are coops the keeper keeps,
The carpenter stirs glue in pots,
And the fire-engine rots.
These I will find and come
To the Solarium
And gaze beyond the wide haha
At loamy parkland stretching far
Whereon the agent contemplates
Dud gates.
All that I ask
Is leave hereon to bask.
Grant me this boon;
Let me have off the afternoon –
The single Wednesday when the crowd
And I may be allowed
To wander here
Year after year.

DANIEL PETTIWARD
Truly Rural, 1939

THE CALL OF THE WILD

CAN gilt alcoves, can marble-mimic gods,
Parterres embroidered, obelisks, and urns
Of high relief; can the long, spreading lake
Or vista lessening to the sight; can Stowe,
With all her Attic fanes, such raptures raise,
As the thrush-haunted copse, where lightly leaps
The fearful fawn the rustling leaves along,
And the brisk squirrel sports from bough to bough,
While from an hollow oak, whose naked roots
O'erhang a pensive rill, the busy bees
Hum drowsy lullabies?

JOSEPH WARTON, *The Enthusiast*, 1744

CURSE on the shrubbery's insipid scenes!
Of tawdry fringe encircling vapid greens;
Where incongruities so well unite,
That nothing can by accident be right;
Thickets that neither shade nor shelter yield;
Yet from the cooling breeze the senses shield:
Prim gravel walks, through which we winding go,
In endless serpentines that nothing show; . . .
  O waft me hence to some neglected vale;
Where, sheltered, I may court the western gale;
And 'midst the gloom which native thickets shed,
Hide from the noontide beams my aching head.

RICHARD PAYNE KNIGHT
The Landscape, 1794

AT CASTLE HOWARD: WATERCOLOUR DRAWING BY J. S. COTMAN, *c.* 1805

COTTAGES AT BURGHCLERE

THE vine
Mantles the little casement; yet the briar
Drops fragrant dew among the July flowers;
And pansies ray'd, and freak'd and mottled pinks
Grow among balm, and rosemary and rue;
There honeysuckles flaunt, and roses low
Almost uncultur'd: some with dark green leaves
Contrast their flowers of pure unsullied white;

PAINTING BY STANLEY SPENCER, R.A., *c.* 1930

Others like velvet robes of regal state
Of richest crimson; while, in thorny moss
Enshrin'd and cradled, the most lovely wear
The hues of youthful beauty's glowing cheek. –
With fond regret I recollect e'en now
In Spring and Summer what delight I felt
Among these cottage gardens. . . .

CHARLOTTE SMITH, *Beachy Head, with Other Poems,* 1807

PARGETTING ON A HOUSE AT CLARE, SUFFOLK: PHOTOGRAPH BY C. RICHTON CAMPIN

WINDOW BOX

WHAT are the casements lin'd with creeping herbs,
The prouder sashes fronted with a range
Of orange, myrtle, or the fragrant weed,
The Frenchman's darling?[1] Are they not all proofs
That man, immur'd in cities, still retains
His inborn inextinguishable thirst
Of rural scenes, compensating his loss
By supplemental shifts, the best he may?
The most unfurnish'd with the means of life,
And they that never pass their brick-wall bounds,
To range the fields and treat their lungs with air,
Yet feel the burning instinct; over head
Suspend their crazy boxes, planted thick
And water'd duly. There the pitcher stands,
A fragment, and the spoutless teapot there:
Sad witnesses how close-pent man regrets
The country, with what ardour he contrives
A peep at Nature, when he can no more.

WILLIAM COWPER, *The Task*, 1785

[1] Mignonette

A GARDEN OF CHILDHOOD

THE stonecrop that on ruins comes
    And hangs like golden balls –
How oft to reach its shining blooms
    We scaled the mossy walls!
And weeds – we gathered weeds as well,
    Of all that bore a flower,
And tied our little posies up
    Beneath the eldern bower.

Our little gardens there we made
    Of blossoms all arow,
And though they had no roots at all
    We hoped to see them grow;
And in the cart-rut after showers
    Of sudden summer rain
We filled our tiny waterpots,
    And cherished them in vain.

JOHN CLARE, *Poems*, 1935
(written *c.* 1830)

TOMORROW'S COWSLIPS

AGAIN the violet of our early days
Drinks beauteous azure from the golden sun,
    And kindles into fragrance at his blaze;
The streams, rejoiced that winter's work is done,
Talk of to-morrow's cowslips, as they run.
    Wild apple, thou art blushing into bloom!
Thy leaves are coming, snowy-blossomed thorn!
    Wake, buried lily! spirit, quit thy tomb;
And thou, shade-loving hyacinth, be born!
Then, haste, sweet rose! sweet woodbine, hymn the morn,
    Whose dew-drops shall illume with pearly light
Each grassy blade that thick embattled stands
    From sea to sea, while daisies infinite
Uplift in praise their little glowing hands
O'er every hill that under heaven expands.

EBENEZER ELLIOTT, *Poetical Works,* 1840

A GREEN PLACE

THE house, too, that gave me shelter must be spoken of; for never have I known any human habitation in a land where people are discovered dwelling in so many secret, green, out-of-the-world places, which had so much of nature in and about it. . . . A small old picturesque red-brick house with high-pitched roof and tall chimneys, a great part of it overrun with ivy and creepers, the walls and tiled roof stained by time and many-coloured lichen to a richly variegated greyish red. The date of the house, cut in a stone tablet in one of the rooms, was 1692. In front there was no lawn, but a walled plot of ground with old, once ornamental trees and bushes symmetrically placed – yews, both spreading and cypress-shaped Irish yew, and tall tapering juniper, and arbor vitae; it was a sort of formal garden which had long thrown off its formality. In a corner of the ground by the side of these dark plants were laurel, syringa, and lilac bushes, and among these such wildings as thorn, elder and bramble had grown up, flourishing greatly, and making of that flowery spot a tangled thicket. At the side of the house there was another plot of ground, grass-grown, which had once been the orchard, and still had a few ancient apple and pear trees, nearly past bearing, with good nesting holes for the tits and starlings in their decayed mossy trunks. . . .

Best of all (for the birds) were the small old half-ruined outhouses which had remained from the distant days when the place, originally a manor, had been turned into a farm-house. They were here and there, scattered about, outside the enclosure, ivy-grown, each looking as old and weather-stained and in harmony with its surroundings as the house itself – the small tumble-down barns, the cow-sheds, the pig-house, the granary with open door and the wooden staircase falling to pieces.

W. H. HUDSON, *Hampshire Days*, 1903

THE FREE SOUL OF THE GARDEN

As I sit there, under the tasselled branch of a larch that leans out from the edge of the shrubbery, I take in afresh the delightful sense of easy abundance, the loose comfort, the soft-bosomed maturity of the garden. Those lobelia-stripes, those marigold-patches, might look harsh and hard, you would think; one knows how smartly odious they can appear in a well-kept garden, so called, where the flowers seem to have been – what shall I say? – to have been stuffed and mounted, lest they should take their ease as living creatures. Not a flower could look constrained, unnaturally smartened, in the garden at Earlham; even if they sat up in rows and stripes, they did so with enjoyment unconcerned. They glowed, they revelled; and more-over it was not, in any vulgar sense, a well-kept garden. It was profusely inconsistent; if one flower-bed was stuck all over with geraniums like a pin-cushion and rimmed with horrible little mon-sters of fretted, empurpled foliage, the next might be a bower, a boscage, a ramp of sweet peas, a bushy luxuriance of phlox and rosemary. And especially the border against the slow curve of the wall which I mentioned just now – this was a mazy confusion of everything that gleams and glows and exhales a spicery of humming fragrance. Peacock butterflies, brilliant red admirals, fluttered over the blue mist of sea-lavender; a tree of verbena, the lemon-scented herb of which you pull a leaf whenever you pass, branched out close to the immense old trunk of the wistaria; salvia blue and red, bitter-sweet phloxes white and crimson-eyed, the russet and purple trum-pets of the lovely creature afflicted with the name of salpiglossis, they all rejoiced together, rambling and crowding in liberal exuberance. The gardener might wreak his worst will, scheming for a smart patchwork; but the free soul of the garden escaped him and bloomed tumultuously.

PERCY LUBBOCK, *Earlham*, 1922

THE IDLE FLOWERS

I HAVE sown upon the fields
Eyebright and Pimpernel,
And Pansy and Poppy-seed
Ripen'd and scatter'd well.

And silver Lady-smock
The meads with light to fill,
Cowslip and Buttercup,
Daisy and Daffodil;

King-cup and Fleur-de-lys
Upon the marsh to meet
With Comfrey, Watermint,
Loose-strife and Meadowsweet;

And all along the stream
My care hath not forgot
Crowfoot's white galaxy
And love's Forget-me-not:

And where high grasses wave
Shall great Moon-daisies blink,
With Rattle and Sorrel sharp
And Robin's ragged pink.

Thick on the woodland floor
Gay company shall be,
Primrose and Hyacinth
And frail Anemone,

Perennial Strawberry-bloom,
Woodsorrel's pencilled veil,
Dishevel'd Willow-weed
And Orchis purple and pale,

Bugle, that blushes blue,
And Woodruff's snowy gem,
Proud Foxglove's finger-bells
And Spurge with milky stem.

High on the downs so bare,
Where thou dost love to climb,
Pink Thrift and Milkwort are,
Lotus and scented Thyme;

And in the shady lanes
Bold Arum's hood of green,
Herb Robert, Violet,
Starwort and Celandine;

And by the dusty road
Bedstraw and Mullein tall,
With red Valerian
And Toadflax on the wall,

Yarrow and Chicory,
That hath for hue no like,
Silene and Mallow mild
And Agrimony's spike,

Blue-eyed Veronicas
And grey-faced Scabious
And downy Silverweed
And striped Convolulus:

Harebell shall haunt the banks,
And thro' the hedgerow peer
Withwind and Snapdragon
And Nightshade's flower of fear.

And where men never sow,
Have I my Thistles set,
Ragwort and stiff Wormwood
And straggling Mignonette

Bugloss and Burdock rank
And prickly Teasel high,
With Umbels yellow and white,
That come to kexes dry.

Pale Chlora shalt thou find,
Sun-loving Centaury,
Cranesbill and Sinjunwort,
Cinquefoil and Betony:

Shock headed Dandelion,
That drank the fire of the sun:
Hawkweed and Marigold,
Cornflower and Campion.

Let Oak and Ash grow strong,
Let Beech her branches spread;
Let Grass and Barley throng
And waving Wheat for bread;

Be share and sickle bright
To labour at all hours;
For thee and thy delight
I have made the idle flowers.

But now 'tis Winter, child,
And bitter northwinds blow,
The ways are wet and wild,
The land is laid in snow.

ROBERT BRIDGES
New Poems
1899

217

STREET SCENE

AND did those feet in ancient time
Walk upon England's mountains green:
And was the holy Lamb of God
On England's pleasant pastures seen?

And did the Countenance Divine
Shine forth upon our clouded hills?
And was Jerusalem builded here
Among these dark Satanic mills?

Bring me my bow of burning gold:
Bring me my arrows of desire:
Bring me my spear: O clouds unfold!
Bring me my chariot of fire!

I will not cease from mental fight,
Nor shall my sword sleep in my hand,
Till we have built Jerusalem
In England's green and pleasant land.

WILLIAM BLAKE, *Milton*, 1804–9

STREET SCENE: PAINTING BY L. S. LOWRY, A.R.A., 1935

A SUNNY DAY: PAINTING BY A. E. MULREADY, 1874

LONDON

'My dear fellow', said Sherlock Holmes, as we sat on either side of the fire in his lodging at Baker Street, '. . . If we could fly out of that window hand in hand, hover over this great city, gently remove the roofs, and peep in at the queer things which are going on, the strange coincidences, the plannings, the cross-purposes, the wonderful chain of events, working through generations, and leading to the most outre results, it would make all fiction with its conventialities and foreseen conclusions most stale and unprofitable.'

SIR ARTHUR CONAN DOYLE

Talking of London, he observed, 'Sir, if you wish to have a just notion of the magnitude of this city, you must not be satisfied with seeing its great streets and squares, but must survey the innumerable little lanes and courts. It is not in the showy evolutions of buildings, but in the multiplicity of human habitations which are crowded together, that the wonderful immensity of London consists.'

SAMUEL JOHNSON, in Boswell's *Life*, 1791

The great sight in London is – London. No man understands himself as an infinitesimal until he has been a drop in that ocean, a grain of sand on that sea margin, a mote in its sunbeam, or the fog or smoke which stands for it; in plainer phrase, a unit among its millions.

OLIVER WENDELL HOLMES

The principal beauty of the Borough of Southwark consists in the prodigious number of its inhabitants.

DANIEL DEFOE

THE COUNTRY TOWN

EVERY town has its own character, invariably English, but always distinctive. Stretched out, as a rule, along some main road, but thickening round the market-place, for generations its interests were parochial, local. Its prosperity hung on the seasons; foreign wars concerned it less than the disputes at the vestry, or than the election, or the fair; the corn crop, or the hops or fruit, mattered to it more than the price of Consols; and somehow, while the restricted but sufficient and simple life of the inhabitants impressed itself unconsciously upon the streets, the townsman as he traversed them breathed its influence unawares, and to this day one feels it. The customary High Street, glistening with reflected sunshine, has a charm beyond that which it derives constantly from the surrounding hills and valleys, and not dependent upon the fresh amplitude of air that enwraps the town so lovingly.

That the nearness of the open country contributes its effect of course is true. Very pleasant it is, as you walk about the old town, to glance through a gap between the houses – down some alley or backway, or under the entrance to an inn-yard – and catch a glimpse of green hillside a mile away under a great vista of sky telling of far horizons. You look up: as likely as not a rook is sailing overhead. You listen; and if the street chances to be quiet you may hear a lark singing. From a street in my own native town I have watched a hawk poised high in air; one spring day I heard, and looking up caught sight of, a passing cuckoo. Many birds are near at hand. Thrushes and blackbirds are melodious in the back gardens, swallows build under the eaves, now and again a wagtail comes down into the roadway. The summer evenings are vocal with the screaming of swifts; in the summer mornings, if you are up early enough, you may see rooks coolly walking in the streets as though they owned them. Pleasant odours come too. There are hours in June when the town is fragrant with the scent of new hay, though you do not see the meadows where it is making. The passing manure-waggon is at worst only half disagreeable, because, after all, it makes you think of farms, and another day the same waggon may bring in for atonement the scent of hops, or of the newly-opened heap of mangold. . . . As you perceive, the shops and dwelling-houses are but a thin screen, a flimsy and often beautiful scene-painting, hiding the open country but not really shutting it out. Rather they frame the sky, and set the imagination dreaming of the fields over which it broods; and while they shut out the eyesores – the neglected farm, the squalid village, or the obtrusively new Cockney villas that too often disfigure the actual country – on the other hand they invite thoughts of the real beauty that lies beyond them. From out there behind the houses and across the valleys comes fancy of coppices full of primroses, hangers fringed with catkins, woodland hollows still open to the April sky, but soon to be curtained in with young leaves. There were never lovelier hedgerows, deeper meadows, more ample downs, or farms more peaceful, than those one is tempted to imagine from the High Street of a country town.

But delicious though all this may be, the street means more than this, and deserves to be looked upon affectionately for its own sake as a feature of the former English country-side. For the old towns – Salisbury and Basingstoke, Lewes, Dunstable, and the hundreds of others whose very names are inspiring – were not in their origin places where rural life ceased; they were the places where it grew tense and vital, and they stand now as a sort of ancient monuments, more interesting than Stonehenge or Old Sarum, of a past dear to every lover of the country.

GEORGE BOURNE, *Lucy Bettesworth*, 1913

COSTER SONG

Oh, tell me in which Gin shop, my dear,
That I shall meet you at Bartlemy Fair,
Oh, tell me at which Gin shop, my dear,
   That I shall meet with thee.

I'll meet thee on September's night,
When the Gin-palace shows a flare-up light
So fine to us but not too bright
   To tell who's lushing there.

You've told me when, now tell me where,
That I shall meet you at Bartlemy Fair;
Where will you blow your cloud, my dear,
   Until I come to thee?

I'll meet you where you know I saw
The donkeys join in sweet He-Haw,
And on Fridays you so oft did draw
   Your Poll on market-day.

You say you'll meet me at Bartlemy Fair,
But how shall I know that you'll be there?
What chi-ock will you tip, my dear,
   That I may know 'tis you?

I'll chaunt aloud that charming air,
That costermongers sing so clear,
All round my hat the green willow I'll wear,
   And then you'll know 'tis me.

NINETEENTH-CENTURY BALLAD

COSTER WOMAN: PAINTING BY CERI RICHARDS, 1943

THE ROYAL CRESCENT, BATH: PAINTING BY FELIX KELLY, 1947

ELEGANT AIR

Of all the gay places the World can afford,
By Gentle and Simple for pastime adored,
Fine balls, and fine concerts, fine buildings, and springs,
Fine walks, and fine views, and a thousand fine things,
Not to mention the sweet situation and air,
What place, my dear Mother, with Bath can compare? . . .
In manners, in dress, in politeness to shine,
O Bath! let the art, let the glory be thine.
I'm sure I have travelled our country all o'er
And ne'er was so civilly treated before . . .
Our neighbour, Sir Easterlin Widgeon, has swore
He ne'er will return to his bogs any more:
The Thickskulls are settled; we've had invitations
With a great many more, on the score of relations.
The Loungers are come, too. Old Stucco has just sent
His plan for a house to be built in the Crescent;
'Twill soon be complete, and they say all their work
Is as strong as St. Paul's, or the Minster at York.
Don't you think 'twould be better to lease our estate,
And buy a good house here before 'tis too late?
You never can go, my dear Mother, where you
So much have to see, and so little to do.

CHRISTOPHER ANSTEY, *The New Bath Guide*, 1766

ILLUSION

ONE late winter afternoon in Oxford Street, amid the noise of vehicles and voices that filled that dusky thoroughfare, as I was borne onward with the crowd past the great electric-lighted shops, a holy Indifference filled my thoughts. Illusion had faded from me; I was not touched by any desire for the goods displayed in the golden windows, nor had I the smallest share in the appetite and fears of all those moving faces. And as I listened with Asiatic detachment to the London traffic, its sound changed into something ancient and dissonant and sad – into the turbid flow of that stream of Craving which sweeps men onward through the meaningless cycles of Existence, blind and enslaved for ever. But I had reached the farther shore, the Harbour of Deliverance, the Holy City; the Great Peace beyond all this turmoil and fret compassed me around. *Om Mani p'adme hum* – I murmured the sacred syllables, smiling with the pitying smile of the Enlightened One on his heavenly lotus.

Then, in a shop-window, I saw a neatly fitted suit-case. I liked that suit-case; I wanted it. Immediately I was enveloped by the mists of Illusion, chained once more to the Wheel of Existence, whirled onward along Oxford Street in that turbid stream of wrong-belief, and lust, and sorrow, and anger.

LOGAN PEARSALL SMITH, *Trivia*, 1918

REALITY

FROM the geyser ventilators
   Autumn winds are blowing down
On a thousand business women
   Having baths in Camden Town.

Waste pipes chuckle into runnels,
   Steam's escaping here and there,
Morning trains through Camden cutting
   Shake the Crescent and the Square.

Early nip of changeful autumn,
   Dahlias glimpsed through garden doors,
At the back precarious bathrooms
   Jutting out from upper floors.

And behind their frail partitions
   Business women lie and soak,
Seeing through the draughty skylight
   Flying clouds and railway smoke.

Rest you there, poor unbelov'd ones,
   Lap your loneliness in heat.
All too soon the tiny breakfast,
   Trolley-bus and windy street!

JOHN BETJEMAN
A Few Late Chrysanthemums, 1954

ST. JAMES'S STREET

Sᴛ. James's Street, of classic fame,
    The finest people throng it.
St. James's Street? I know the name!
    I think I've passed along it!
Why, that's where Sacharissa sighed
    When Waller read his ditty;
Where Byron lived, and Gibbon died,
    And Alvanley was witty.

A famous street! To yonder Park
    Young Churchill stole in class-time;
Come, gaze on fifty men of mark,
    And then recall the past time!
The *plats* at White's, the play at Crocks',
    The bumpers to Miss Gunning;
The *bonhomie* of Charlie Fox,
    And Selwyn's ghastly funning . . .

I like the haunts of Old Cockaigne
    Where wit and wealth were squandered,
The halls that tell of hoop and train,
    Where grace and rank have wandered –
Those halls where ladies fair and leal
    First ventured to adore me! –
Something of that old love I feel
    For this old street before me.

FREDERICK LOCKER-LAMPSON
London Lyrics, 1876

SUBURBAN PASTORALS

HERE, the surface of things is certainly humdrum, the streets dingy, the green places, where the child goes a-maying, tame enough. But nowhere are things more apt to respond to the brighter weather, nowhere is there so much difference between rain and sunshine, nowhere do the clouds roll together more grandly; those quaint suburban pastorals gathering a certain quality of grandeur from the background of the great city, with its weighty atmosphere, and portent of storm in the rapid light on dome and bleached stone steeples.

WALTER PATER, *Appreciations*, 1889

LIFTING through the broken clouds there shot
A searching beam of golden sunset-shine.
It swept the town allotments, plot by plot,
And all the digging clerks became divine –
Stood up like heroes with their spades of brass,
Turning the ore that made the realms of Spain!
So shone they for a moment. Then, alas!
The cloud-rift closed; and they were clerks again.

RICHARD CHURCH
The Dream and Other Poems, 1927

LONDON SPRING

THE rounded buses loom through softest blue,
The pavement smells of dust but of narcissus too,
The awnings stretch like petals in the sun,
And even the oldest taxis glitter as they run.

Over the sooted secret garden walls
As in another Eden cherry-blossom falls,
Lithe under shadowing lilacs steal the cats,
And even the oldest ladies tilt their summery hats.

FRANCES CORNFORD, *Travelling Home*, 1948

AUTUMN IN HYDE PARK

THE beeches' copper islands float
Suspended in the mellow woods,
Where autumn substitutes for words
A private dictionary of moods.

The red and russet-throated birds
Describe in avenues of love
Circles of a yellow grief
Narrowed in the plane tree's leaf.

The rowan's scarlet statement burns
A sudden presage of the doom
That strips the naked falling bark
White in the amber gloom.

The lake conveys the quiet pause
Between the sable splash of oars,
As underfoot the horses' hooves
Trample the images of larks.

The evening's traffic soon dilates
Smoky spirals in its lights,
And twists the plaster-coloured
Mist into honeyed fumes of night.

Then ruins echo unheard noise
As darkness drifts like tepid breath,
Printing on the season's hearse
The black letters of its death.

ALAN ROSS, *Something of the Sea*, 1954

MORNING AT THE WINDOW

THEY are rattling breakfast plates in basement kitchens,
And along the trampled edges of the street
I am aware of the damp souls of housemaids
Sprouting despondently at area gates.

The brown waves of fog toss up to me
Twisted faces from the bottom of the street,
And tear from a passer-by with muddy skirts
An aimless smile that hovers in the air
And vanishes along the level of the roofs.

T. S. ELIOT
Prufrock and Other Observations, 1917

NDON STREET IN SNOW: PAINTING BY HAROLD GILMAN, 1917

LONDON FROM
WATERLOO BRID◉
TEMPERA
PAINTING BY
C. R. W. NEVINSO

SEAGULLS ON THE SERPENTINE

MEMORY, out of the mist, in a long slow ripple
    Breaks, blindly, against the shore.
The mist has buried the town in its own oblivion.
    This, this is the sea once more.

Mist – mist – brown mist: but a sense in the air of snow-flakes!
    I stand where the ripples die,
Lift up an arm and wait, till my lost ones know me,
    Wheel overhead, and cry.

Salt in the eyes, and the seagulls, mewing and swooping,
    Snatching the bread from my hand;
Brushing my hand with their breasts, in swift caresses
    To show that they understand.

Oh, why are you so afraid? We are all of us exiles!
    Wheel back in your clamorous rings!
We have all of us lost the sea, and we all remember.
    But you – have wings.

ALFRED NOYES, *Collected Poems*, 1927

ENVOI

Mother of holy fire! Mother of holy dew!
Thy children of the mist, the moor, the mountain side,
These change not from thine heart, these to thine heart allied:
These, that rely on thee, as blossoms on the blue.
O passionate, dark faces, melancholy's hue!
O deep, grey eyes, so tragic with the fires they hide!
Sweet Mother, in whose light these live! thou dost abide,
Star of the West, pale to the world: these know thee true.

No alien hearts may know that magic, which acquaints
Thy soul with splendid passion, a great fire of dreams;
Thine heart with lovelier sorrow, than the wistful sea.
Voices of Celtic singers and of Celtic Saints
Live on the ancient air: their royal sunlight gleams
On moorland Merioneth and on sacred Dee.

LIONEL JOHNSON, 'Wales'
Poems, 1895

In the highlands, in the country places,
Where the old plain men have rosy faces,
   And the young fair maidens
      Quiet eyes;
Where essential silence cheers and blesses,
And for ever in the hill-recesses
   Her more lovely music
      Broods and dies.

O to mount again where erst I haunted;
Where the old red hills are bird-enchanted,
   And the low green meadows
      Bright with sward;
And when even dies, the million-tinted,
And the night has come, and planets glinted,
   Lo, the valley, hollow
      Lamp-bestarred.

O to dream, O to awake and wander
There, and with delight to take and render,
   Through the trance of silence,
      Quiet breath!
Lo! for there, among the flowers and grasses,
Only the mightier movement sounds and passes;
   Only winds and rivers,
      Life and death.

ROBERT LOUIS STEVENSON, *Songs of Travel*, 1896

O THAT I were
Where breaks the pure cold light
On English hills
And pewits rising cry,
And gray is all the sky.

Or at evening there
When the faint slow light stays,
And far below
Sleeps the last lingering sound
And night leans all round.

O then, O there
'Tis English haunted ground.
The diligent stars
Creep out, watch, and smile;
The wise moon lingers awhile.

For surely there
Heroic shapes are moving,
Visible thoughts,
Passions, things divine,
Clear beneath clear star-shine. . . .

JOHN FREEMAN, 'English Hills'
Stone Trees, 1916

M

NOTES ON THE ILLUSTRATIONS

The names of the owners of works illustrated are printed in italics

Frontispiece. BILSTON ENAMEL PATCH BOXES. *c. 1800. Ipswich, Christchurch Mansion.*

17. NICHOLAS POCOCK (1741–1821). Nelson's Flagships (Detail). 1807. Oil on panel. 14×21 in. *Greenwich, National Maritime Museum.*

    The illustration shows half of a commemorative painting of four of the ships in which Nelson served. The *Victory*, Nelson's flagship from 1803 to 1805, is in the foreground. Beyond her is the *Captain*, in which he served in 1796–7.

18. EDWARD WADSWORTH, A.R.A. (1889–1949). Signals. 1942. Tempera on canvas. 40×28 in. *London, Tate Gallery.*

21. LIVERPOOL DELFT PUNCH BOWL. *c. 1760.* 14 in. diameter. *Cambridge, Fitzwilliam Museum.*

22. JOHN BRETT, A.R.A. (1830–1902). February in the Isle of Wight. 1866. Watercolour and body colour. $15\frac{3}{8} \times 13\frac{7}{16}$ in. *Birmingham Art Gallery.*

    Brett, for whose work Ruskin had a great admiration, was much influenced by the Pre-Raphaelites, but applied their principles to actual landscape instead of myth and allegory.

27. JOHN TUNNARD (*b.* 1900). Weather Forecast. 1945. Oil on panel. 24×22 in. *Sir David Scott, K.C.M.G.*

28. STAFFORDSHIRE POTTERY GROUP. The Sailor's Return. *c.* 1840. 12½ in. high. *Mrs Robert Bevan.*

37. EDWARD ARDIZZONE (*b.* 1900). Southend (Detail). 1955. Watercolour drawing. 18 × 24½ in. *Sir Colin Anderson.*

38. PHILIP WILSON STEER, R.A. (1860–1942). The Pier Head, Walberswick. 1888. Oil on canvas. 36 × 36 in. *Hugo Pitman, Esq.*

43. JOHN SELL COTMAN (1782–1842). The Devil's Elbow. Rokeby. *c.* 1807. Watercolour. 17¾ × 13⅞ in. *Norwich, Castle Museum.*
   One of a group of drawings, of which 'Greta Bridge' is the best known, done during the happiest days of Cotman's clouded life, whilst he was visiting his friends the Cholmeleys in Yorkshire.

44. SAMUEL PALMER (1805–81). The Bright Cloud. *c.* 1831. Drawing in Indian ink. 6 × 6 in. *London, British Museum.*
   This is one of several drawings done by Palmer from which his painting 'The Bright Cloud' was elaborated some four years later. It has that visionary intensity which derived from his contact with Blake.

49. LAURENCE WHISTLER (*b.* 1907). Stonehenge. Diamond-point engraving on glass. 1955. 9 in. high. *Sir Hugh Dawson.*

50. JOHN PIPER (*b.* 1903). Bolsover. 1944. Watercolour. 26 × 21 in. *Sir Osbert Sitwell, Bt.*
   Bolsover Castle, Derbyshire, was built by William Peveril in the eleventh century, but rebuilt by Sir Charles Cavendish in 1613-17. It is now partly in ruins.

59. JOHN CONSTABLE, R.A. (1776–1837). Barges on the Stour, Dedham Church in the Distance. *c.* 1810. Oil on paper on canvas. 10¼ × 12¼ in. *London, Victoria and Albert Museum.*

60. WEDGWOOD POTTERY. Trial pieces made for the Imperial Russian dinner service. 1774. *Messrs Josiah Wedgwood & Sons Ltd.* This famous dinner service, made by Josiah Wedgwood for the Empress Catherine, and still to be seen in Russia, consisted of some 1,200 pieces each with a 'real view from English Gardens and pleasure grounds painted in enamel'.

73. THOMAS GIRTIN (1775–1802). Tintern Abbey. Watercolour. 13¾ × 11 in. *Manchester, Whitworth Art Gallery.*

74–75. FRANCIS TOWNE (1740–1816). Ambleside. 1786. Water-colour. 6½ × 18½ in. *Herbert Powell Collection of Early British Watercolours.*

76. DOLL'S HOUSE. Nostell Priory, Yorkshire. Eighteenth century. *Major the Hon. R. D. G. Winn.* The scale of the model is indicated by the 5-ft. screen beside it.

89. THOMAS ROWLANDSON (1756–1827). Entrance to a Village. Watercolour. 11⅝ × 15⅛ in. *London, Victoria and Albert Museum.*

90. JOHN WHITE ABBOTT (1763–1851). Corra Lynn, on the Clyde. 1791. Watercolour. 9½ × 7½ in. *London, Victoria and Albert Museum.* Abbott, an Exeter man who practised as a surgeon and never sold any of his pictures, was a pupil of Francis Towne (*see plate on pages 74–5*).

99. RICHARD WILSON, R.A. (1713–82). Snowdon from Llyn Nantlle. *c.* 1766. Oil on canvas. 39½ × 50 in. *Liverpool, Walker Art Gallery.*

This view of Snowdon – 'as magnificent as it is faithful', according to Pennant in his *Tour of Wales*, 1783 – is perhaps the masterpiece of Wilson's paintings of Wales in his 'classical' manner. There is another version of it in the Nottingham Art Gallery.

100. WOOD CARVING. A Wooseman. Fifteenth century. Photograph by Frederick Bantick. *Long Melford, The Bull Inn.*

Carved at the head of one of the timbers in the fifteenth-century inn at Long Melford, in Suffolk, this vigorous figure represents a Wooseman, the traditional 'Green Man' or 'Man of the Woods'.

105. ROUNDABOUT. Photograph by Edwin Smith.

106. EDWARD BAWDEN, R.A. (b. 1903). Agricultural Show. 1947. Watercolour drawing. *Hulton Press.*

115. TRISTRAM HILLIER (b. 1905). A Farm Waggon. 1943. Oil on canvas. 6 × 9 in. *Captain Burgess Meredith.*

116–117. THOMAS GAINSBOROUGH, R.A. (1727–88). Mr and Mrs Robert Andrews. *c.* 1749. Oil on canvas. 27½ × 47 in. *G. W. Andrews, Esq.*

Robert Andrews, of Auberies, Bulmer, Suffolk, married Frances Mary Carter, of Ballingdon House, Sudbury, in 1748. This picture, which shows the tower of St Peter's, Sudbury, in the background, was probably painted soon after their marriage.

118. JOHN NASH, R.A. (b. 1893). Threshing. 1915. Oil on canvas 30 × 25 in. *Lance Sieveking, Esq.*

127. PAUL NASH (1889–1946). Oxenbridge Pond. 1928. Oil on canvas. 39¼ × 34½ in. *Birmingham Art Gallery.*

128. SIR ANTHONY VAN DYCK (1599–1641). Landscape. *c.* 1635. Watercolour drawing. 10½ × 8½ in. *London, British Museum.*
This delicate and poetic composition of light greens and blues was drawn by Van Dyck after he settled in England in 1632.

133. PAUL SANDBY MUNN (1773–1845). Fountains Abbey. Watercolour. 13 × 10⅜ in. *Manchester, Whitworth Art Gallery.*
A godson of Paul Sandby, Munn was a member of the Old Water Colour Society, a minor figure with a peculiar sensibility to the beauty of ruins.

134. JOHN SELL COTMAN (1782–1842). Breaking the Clod. *c.* 1807. Monochrome drawing. 12½ × 10½ in. *London, British Museum.*

143. JOHN CROME (1768–1821). Landscape with Cottages. Watercolour. 20½ × 16¾ in. *London, Victoria and Albert Museum.*

144. IVON HITCHENS (b. 1893). Landscape in Essex (Detail). 1946. Oil on canvas. 19½ × 41¾ in. *Liverpool, Walker Art Gallery.*
The detail shown is the right-hand half of the picture.

149. SIR WILLIAM NICHOLSON (1872–1949). Wiltshire Pastoral. Oil on canvas board. 12½ × 15½ in. *Mrs H. M. Drew.*
Painted when the artist was living at Sutton Veny, after 1923.

150. ALAN REYNOLDS (b. 1926). Studies of Barley for 'Young September's Cornfield'. 1954. Wash drawing. 16 × 11¼ in. *Redfern Gallery.*

155. ELEAZAR ALBIN:(*fl.* 1713–59). Poplar Hawk Moth. Hand-coloured engraving from *A Natural History of English Insects,* 1720. Albin was a drawing-master who produced the first comprehensive – if unscientific – illustrated handbook of English insects.

156. LIVERPOOL DELFT POTTERY DISH. *c.* 1750. Tin-glazed earthenware. 12½ in. diameter. *London, Victoria and Albert Museum.*

165. THE BRADFORD TABLE CARPET (DETAIL). Elizabethan. Linen canvas embroidered with silks in tent stitch. *London, Victoria and Albert Museum.*
     The illustration shows a detail, about 17 in. high, from the edge of this famous table covering (the whole measures about 10½ × 5½ feet) which came from the Earl of Bradford's collection at Castle Bromwich Hall.

166. PETER L. PERI (b. 1899). The Tackle. 1953. Sculpture in concrete. 24 in. high. *The Artist.*
     Exhibited by the Football Association, 1953.

171. SIR GEORGE CHALMERS (died 1791). William St Clair of Roslin, Captain of the Honourable Company of Edinburgh Golfers, 1761, 1766, 1770 and 1771. Oil on canvas. 88 × 61 in. *Edinburgh: The Royal Company of Archers.*

172. SPENCER FREDERICK GORE (1878–1914). The Cricket Match. 1909. Oil on canvas. 20×24 in. *Wakefield, City Art Gallery.*
Spencer Gore, whose work until recently has been somewhat underestimated, was one of the chief figures – and perhaps the most original – in the Camden Town Group. Another member was Harold Gilman (*see* plate on p. 235).

177. WILLIAM POWELL FRITH, R.A. (1819–1909). The Fair Toxophilites. 1872. Oil on canvas. 37¾ × 31½ in. *Mrs Edgar Sheppard.*
The models for this painting were three of the painter's daughters. The present owner is the daughter of the lady standing on the right.

178. DETAIL OF OLD FORD PRINTED COTTON CURTAIN. 1769. *London, Victoria and Albert Museum.*
A fine example of English cotton-printing, done in purple from an engraved plate, and over-printed in colours by means of wood-blocks. Signed and dated by the printer, Robert Jones, who had a factory at Old Ford, near Bow, until 1780.

183. VICTORIAN WALLPAPER PATTERN. Salmon Fishing in the Highlands. *c.* 1870. *London, Victoria and Albert Museum.*
This panel of machine-printed wallpaper comes from the gun-room of Blatherwycke Hall, Peterborough.

184–185. GEORGE STUBBS, A.R.A. (1724–1806). Gimcrack. *c.* 1765. Oil on canvas. 40×76 in. *Major and the Hon. Mrs R. Macdonald-Buchanan.*
Gimcrack, the famous racehorse which gave its name to the Gimcrack Stakes, at York, and the Gimcrack Club in New York, is here seen near the Rubbing House at Newmarket, and again, in the background, winning a race on the Heath. The jockey on foot is wearing the colours of Gimcrack's owner, Lord Bolingbroke.

186. SIR ALFRED MUNNINGS, P.P.R.A. (b. 1878). Belvoir Hounds walking out in the Park. 1920–21. Oil on canvas. 30×36 in. *Major T. Bouch.* Reproduction by kind permission of Messrs Frost & Reed.

191. FRANCIS WHEATLEY (1747–1801). A Sportsman and his Son. Oil on canvas. 36×28 in. Photograph by courtesy of Messrs Thomas Agnew & Sons. *New York, Private Collection.*

192. DERBY PORCELAIN GROUP. A Sportsman and a Lady. *c.* 1750. 5¾ in. high. *London, British Museum.*

197. ADAM BUCK (*fl.* 1795–1834). Skating Lovers. Aquatint by Piercy Roberts and J. C. Stadler. 1800. *London, British Museum.*

198. EMBROIDERED PICTURE, GARDEN SCENE. Early eighteenth century. Satin, embroidered with coloured silks in long and short, split and satin stitches, with couched work. 13¼ × 12¾ in. *London, Victoria and Albert Museum.*

207. JOHN SELL COTMAN (1782–1842). At Castle Howard. *c.* 1805. Sepia drawing. 8½ × 6¼ in. *London, Victoria and Albert Museum.*

208–209. STANLEY SPENCER, R.A. (b. 1891). Cottages at Burghclere. *c.* 1930. Oil on canvas. 24½ × 63 in. *Cambridge, Fitzwilliam Museum.*
   The artist lived at Burghclere from 1927 to 1932 whilst working on the decoration of the Memorial Chapel.

210. PARGETTING ON A HOUSE AT CLARE, SUFFOLK. Seventeenth century. Photograph by C. Richton Campin.

219. LAURENCE STEPHEN LOWRY, A.R.A. (b. 1887). Street Scene. 1935. Oil on canvas. 21×15 in. *Howard Spring, Esq.*

220. A. E. MULREADY (d. 1886). A Sunny Day. 1874. Oil on canvas. 30×20 in. *Mrs Field.*

225. CERI RICHARDS (b. 1903). Coster woman. 1943. Ink, chalk and gouache on paper. 11×7¾ in. *Sir Colin Anderson.*

226. FELIX KELLY (b. 1916). The Royal Crescent, Bath. 1947. Oil on panel. 13×9 in. *Hulton Press.*

235. HAROLD GILMAN (1876–1919). London Street in Snow. 1917. Oil on canvas. 19½×15½. *Miss Elizabeth Arnold.*
Gilman, who died during the influenza epidemic of 1919, was with Spencer Gore, one of the group of painters surrounding Sickert in Fitzroy Street.

236. CHRISTOPHER RICHARD WYNNE NEVINSON (1889–1946). London from Waterloo Bridge, Winter. Tempera on panel. 30×20 in. *London Museum.*

Endpapers. THE BRADFORD TABLE CARPET. A larger section of the subject reproduced in colour on page 165.

ACKNOWLEDGEMENTS

THE COMPILER AND PUBLISHERS make acknowledgement of the generous facilities afforded by the galleries, artists and collectors named in the Notes on the Illustrations. Almost all the works reproduced in colour were specially photographed for this book by Fine Art Engravers, and the compiler wishes to thank the photographers, Mr John Webb and Miss Eileen Tweedy, for their skilful collaboration. He would also like to acknowledge particularly the help and information provided by Sir Colin Anderson, Mr G. W. Andrews, Major Alastair C. Blair, of the Royal Company of Archers, Miss Brigid Bodkin, of the Birmingham Art Gallery, Mr Ralph Fastnedge, of the Walker Art Gallery, Liverpool, Mr John Hayward, Mr F. W. Hawcroft, of the Castle Museum, Norwich, Mr C. H. Gibbs-Smith, of the Victoria and Albert Museum, Miss Margaret Pilkington, of the Whitworth Art Gallery, Manchester, Mr Hugo Pitman, Sir David Scott, Mr Howard Spring, Mr Norman Smedley, of the Ipswich Museum and Art Gallery, and Mr John Wedgwood.

For permission to print copyright passages acknowledgement is made to the Architectural Press for a passage from *The Castles on the Ground* by Mr J. M. Richards; to Mr Edmund Blunden for four poems, and passages from *Cricket Country* and *Votive Tablets*; to Mr Gerald Bullett and Messrs Michael Joseph for a poem from *Windows on a Vanished Time*; to the Cambridge University Press for a passage from *The Wheelwright's Shop* by George Sturt; to Messrs Jonathan Cape for a poem from *Of Period and Place* by Mr John Arlott and a passage from *Earlham* by Mr Percy Lubbock; to Mr Richard Church and Messrs J. M. Dent & Sons for two poems; to the Clarendon Press for a poem by Robert Bridges; to Messrs Collins for a poem by E. B. Osborn, and a passage from *Cities and Sea Coasts* by Arthur Symons; to Messrs Constable for two passages from *Trivia* by Logan Pearsall Smith; to the Cresset Press for poems by Mrs Frances Cornford; to Mr Walter de la Mare and Messrs Faber & Faber for four poems; to Messrs J. M. Dent & Sons for passages from *The Mirror of the Sea* and *The Nigger of the Narcissus* by Joseph Conrad, from *Coming Down the Wye* by Mr Robert Gibbings, from *Hampshire Days* and *Nature in Downland* by W. H. Hudson, from *The South Country* by Edward Thomas, and from *Quite Early One Morning* by Dylan Thomas; to the executors of Austin Dobson for a poem from *At the Sign of the Lyre*; to Messrs Gerald Duckworth for passages from *Lucy Bettesworth* and *Memoirs of a Surrey Labourer* by George Bourne; to Messrs Faber & Faber for poems by Mr T. S. Eliot and Dr Edwin Muir; to Messrs B. Feldman & Company for 'Beside the Seaside'; to Mrs John Freeman for a poem by John Freeman; to Dr Philip Gosse for a poem by Sir Edmund Gosse; to the executors of Rudyard Kipling and Messrs Methuen for extracts from a poem by Rudyard Kipling; to Mr Osbert Lancaster; to Messrs John Lane, the Bodley Head, for a passage from *Corduroy* by Mr Adrian Bell; to Professor C. Day Lewis for a poem; to Messrs Longmans Green for passages from *Clio, A Muse* by Dr G. M. Trevelyan and *A Gardener's Year* by Sir H. Rider Haggard, and a poem by Andrew Lang; to Messrs Macmillan and the Trustees of the Hardy Estate for a poem by Thomas Hardy; to Dr John Masefield, O.M., the Society of Authors and Messrs Macmillan for a passage from *A Tarpaulin Muster*; to Messrs Methuen & Company for a passage from *No Boats on the River* by Sir Alan Herbert; to Messrs John Murray for poems by Mr John Betjeman; to Mr Alfred Noyes for a poem; to the Oxford University Press for poems by Gerard Manley Hopkins; to Mr J. B. Priestley and Messrs William Heinemann for passages from *The Balconinny* and *The Good Companions*; to the proprietors of *Punch* for poems by Mr Daniel Pettiward; to Messrs Putnam for a poem by Sir William S. Gilbert; to Mr Alan Ross for three poems; to the Hon. V. Sackville-West and Messrs William Heinemann for passages from *The Land*; to Mr Siegfried Sassoon and Messrs Faber & Faber for a poem, and a passage from *The Weald of Youth*; to Messrs Sidgwick & Jackson for a poem by John Drinkwater; to Sir Osbert Sitwell, Bt, and Messrs Macmillan for passages from *Right Hand, Left Hand*; to Mr Sacheverell Sitwell and Messrs Duckworth for a passage from *Canons of Giant Art*; to Mrs Edward Thomas for poems by Edward Thomas; to the Unicorn Press for a poem by Lionel Johnson; and to Mr Leonard Woolf for a passage from *Kew Gardens* by Virginia Woolf.

INDEX OF AUTHORS AND ARTISTS

INDEX OF AUTHORS AND ARTISTS

FANE, JULIAN (1827–70), 47
Freeman, John (1880–1929), 240
Frith, William Powell (1819–1909), 177

GAINSBOROUGH, THOMAS (1727–88),
116, 117
Gibbings, Robert (b. 1889), 72
Gilbert, Sir William Schwenk (1836–
1911), 122
Gilman, Harold (1876–1919), 235
Girtin, Thomas (1775–1802), 73
Glover-Kind, John A., 13
Gore, Spencer Frederick (1878–1914),
172
Gosse, Sir Edmund (1849–1928), 111
Grahame, Rev. James (1765–1811),
88, 180
Gray, David (1838–61), 93, 153
Green, Matthew (1696–1737), 189

HAGGARD, SIR HENRY RIDER (1856–
1925), 124
Hardy, Thomas (1840–1928), 126
Hawker, Rev. Robert Stephen (1803–
75), 45
Hazlitt, William (1778–1830), 103,
163, 200
Herbert, Sir Alan Patrick (b. 1890), 25
Hillier, Tristram (b. 1905), 115
Hitchens, Ivon (b. 1893), 144
Holmes, Oliver Wendell (1809–94),
221
Hollond, John, 19
Hood, Thomas (1799–1845), 146
Hopkins, Gerard Manley (1844–89),
146, 151, 157
Horne, Richard Henry (1803–84), 92
Howitt, William (1792–1879), 174
Hudson, William Henry (1841–1922),
147, 214

Hurdis, Rev. James (1763–1801), 84,
142

JEFFERIES, RICHARD (1848–1887), 110
Johnson, Lionel (1867–1902), 238
Johnson, Samuel (1709–84), 221
Jones, Ebenezer (1820–60), 137

KEBLE, REV. JOHN (1792–1866), 125
Kelly, Felix (b. 1916), 226
Kingsley, Rev. Charles (1819–75), 98
Kipling, Rudyard (1865–1936), 31
Knight, Richard Payne (1750–1824),
51, 204

LANCASTER, OSBERT (b. 1908), 77
Lang, Andrew (1844–1912), 68
Leigh, Dr Charles (1662–1701?), 203
Lewis, Cecil Day (b. 1904), 58
Locker-Lampson, Frederick (1821–
95), 230
Lowry, Laurence Stephen (b. 1887),
219
Lubbock, Percy (b. 1879), 215

MARTIN, ADMIRAL SIR THOMAS BYAM
(1773–1854), 14
Masefield, John (b. 1875), 20
Moir, David Macbeth (1798–1851),
95
Moore, Thomas (1779–1852), 163
Muir, Edwin (b. 1887), 30
Mulready, A. E. (d. 1886), 220
Munn, Paul Sandby (1773–1845), 133
Munnings, Sir Alfred (b. 1878), 186

NASH, JOHN (b. 1893), 118
Nash, Paul (1889–1946), 127
Nevinson, Christopher Richard
Wynne (1889–1946), 236

254